Date Due

OCT 4 1983

# THE COOL ARM
## OF DESTRUCTION

# THE
# COOL ARM
# OF
# DESTRUCTION

## Modern Weapons
## and
## Moral Insensitivity

by
ROBERT W. GARDINER

THE WESTMINSTER PRESS
Philadelphia

Copyright © 1974 The Westminster Press

Book Design by Dorothy Alden Smith

Published by The Westminster Press ®
Philadelphia, Pennsylvania

PRINTED IN THE UNITED STATES OF AMERICA

**Library of Congress Cataloging in Publication Data**

Gardiner, Robert W., 1932–
    The cool arm of destruction.

    Bibliography: p.
    1. Atomic warfare—Moral and religious aspects.
I. Title.
BR115.A85G37                    261.8′73                    74–4351
ISBN 0–664–20701–4

To my son Matthew

In the hope that there will be a future—
for him and for all the children of men

There are many cumbersome ways to kill a man.
You can make him carry a plank of wood
to the top of a hill and nail him to it. To do this
properly you require a crowd of people
wearing sandals, a cock that crows, a cloak
to dissect, a sponge, some vinegar and one
man to hammer the nails home.

Or you can take a length of steel,
shaped and chased in a traditional way,
and attempt to pierce the metal cage he wears.
But for this you need white horses,
English trees, men with bows and arrows,
at least two flags, a prince and a
castle to hold your banquet in.

Dispensing with nobility, you may, if the wind
allows, blow gas at him. But then you need
a mile of mud sliced through with ditches,
not to mention black boots, bomb craters,
more mud, a plague of rats, a dozen songs
and some round hats made of steel.

In an age of aeroplanes, you may fly
miles above your victim and dispose of him by
pressing one small switch. All you then
require is an ocean to separate you, two
systems of government, a nation's scientists,
several factories, a psychopath and
land that no one needs for several years.

These are, as I began, cumbersome ways
to kill a man. Simpler, direct, and much more neat
is to see that he is living somewhere in the middle
of the twentieth century, and leave him there.

—*Edwin Brock*

—"Five Ways to Kill a Man," from
*With Love from Judas,* by Edwin
Brock. Reprinted by permission of
Scorpion Press in *Where Steel
Winds Blow,* ed. by Robert Cromie;
copyright 1968 by Robert Cromie;
published by David McKay Com-
pany, Inc.

# CONTENTS

# PREFACE

SOMEWHERE ABOUT 1960, I GOT CONVERTED. FROM TIME TO
time I had seen bombers making their vapor trails in
the sky, and from these occurrences I had derived the sense
of security which official ideology suggested I should. It
seemed clear, at the time, that one thing, and one thing
alone, stood between us and the utter destruction of everything that makes human life decent: the deterrent power of
the Big Bomb. It had not occurred to me, as yet, that the
defense of humane values (read: "our way of life") by
means of weapons whose victims would be numbered in
the scores of millions might be a shade less than totally
moral, rational, or "realistic."

Yet, as the decade of the 1950's came to a close, it
dawned upon me, as it has upon many others, that the
mutual brandishing of megatonnage by two hostile and
rather intolerant superpowers might *not* be, despite official
assurances, the best means of guaranteeing either the survival or the fundamental humanity of the race. In fact, it
occurred to me, in the strongest possible way, that there
is no conceivable human objective that could justify the
use, or the threatened use, of nuclear weapons by one
people against another. I have not, in the intervening

period, had any reason to change my views. On several occasions, I have seen us come within a hair's breadth of Armageddon, wondering all the while how many narrow escapes we can manage before we make that one last big Mistake. I have seen the nuclear arsenal, initially powerful enough to exterminate whole peoples, increase in a few years by several thousand percent. I have seen learned scholars project scenarios of apocalyptic violence and debate soberly how many millions of deaths would be "acceptable" in the event of a nuclear conflict. I have seen, for ten years, in Southeast Asia the nearly total devastation that can now be inflicted on a people even by means of "conventional" weapons. None of these things have enhanced my confidence in the efficacy of armed violence, nuclear or otherwise, as the road to anything remotely resembling peace.

I cannot, without serious reservation, call myself a pacifist. Yet, to one who has lived through the dreadful decade of the 1960's there is no possible relationship between the carefully circumscribed use of force as a defense of basic human justice and the obscenely grotesque dimensions assumed by organized violence in the modern world. The fate of Indochina, virtually destroyed as a viable human society, and the ever-present specter of nuclear suicide which hangs over the race may suggest that the whole system of organized violence as presently constituted is at last shown to be morally bankrupt as a means of "defending" anything. In his famous address at M.I.T. in the late 1960's, Dr. George Wald commented that the present generation of students is not sure if it has any future. I can think of no more telling epitaph for a policy whose publicly stated objective was to guarantee our "security."

To speak of modern weapons as a moral problem is to speak of what they do, or would do, to the people they hit. It is also, and with equal importance, to speak of what they have done to the rest of us. The dead and the maimed, the sorrowing and the embittered, are not the only victims of the weaponry of mass destruction. Its principal victims —namely, ourselves—remain physically untouched. Nothing betrays our crippling so vividly as the way our moral perceptions have been altered by the impact of technologized and apocalyptic violence made increasingly routine. What men think and feel determines what they do; it may be less obvious, but no less important, that what men do—or plan to do—determines what they think and feel. This rule imposes a logic from which there is no escape. It catches within its grip those who, in the enclaves of government-sponsored scholarship, plan scenarios of violence which they cannot possibly comprehend in human terms. It catches those who, attaching their brains and bodies to machines of almost limitless power, are able at the mere flick of a switch, and with scarcely a trace of personal involvement, to wreak violence of cosmic proportions upon countless unseen victims half a world away. It catches those who by their apathy and their willingness to leave to the "experts" the issue of how men live and die have permitted the growth of a political morality in which any level of violence is "acceptable" so long as it (1) appears to serve the national interest, and (2) occurs at sufficient distance from ourselves to spare us the moral agony of having to face in any serious way the consequences of our decisions.

In the ancient wisdom of the race there is an evident awareness that the human drive toward power contains a dreadful ambiguity. Man, who by appropriating the secret forces of nature is given the power to create, is by that fact also given the power to create *monsters*. The ancient wisdom foretells the modern reality: we have created a monster. In turn, the monster has re-created his master: we have begun to resemble him. Our bondage to the machinery of apocalypse has profoundly corrupted our moral consciousness. If we are not to suffer a further attenuation of our basic humanity, we shall have to admit what has happened to us already, and recognize that we can no longer stake the defense of human values in this world on what are essentially instruments of genocide.

R.W.G.

# 1.

# POWER UNLIMITED:
# A NEW PROBLEM FOR A NEW TIME

THOUGHTFUL MEN RECOGNIZE THAT THE HUMAN RACE TODAY
faces a challenge which in many respects is unlike any
ever faced before. This challenge, in its ultimate form, is
simply: whether we shall or shall not survive as a species.
These rather startling alternatives confront us as the product of a radically new situation. Its substance may be
defined by the reality of power: of this resource, we now
possess enough to wipe ourselves, in a matter of hours,
entirely off the face of the planet. Man has always been a
seeker of power. Yet, what distinguishes his present condition is not the aim but the achievement. The Promethean
dream of omnipotence has at last come within a hair's
breadth of being true—and we have discovered that its
possession is by no means an unambiguous blessing.

Possession of power, in the magnitude now accessible,
has made possible new kinds of weapons, and thus a new
kind of warfare, a warfare whose end product is potentially
total destruction of the combatant societies—and quite
possibly of the human race itself. The systematic pulveriz-
ing of Germany and Japan during World War II, as well
as the more recent assault on the land and people of Indochina, has shown that such an objective is approachable

even with "conventional" weapons, if diligently applied. Yet with the weapons that are now available, such destruction as this could be duplicated and multiplied hundreds of times over in every major nation within a matter of hours.

The nature and power of nuclear weapons are too well known by now to require extended commentary. What is most difficult to comprehend is the extent of the transition that has taken place during the past quarter century. The standard aerial weapon of World War II, the blockbuster, contained somewhat more than twenty thousand pounds of TNT. The two atomic bombs that fell on Japan at the end of the war each multiplied that power by more than 1,000 times. Yet, within seven or eight years, new (thermonuclear) weapons were developed that multiplied the power of the atomic bomb by an *additional* factor of 1,000. Today standard strategic weapons carry, as a rule, the equivalent of anywhere from one to twenty million tons of TNT.[1] The total nuclear stockpiles of both the United States and Soviet Russia, taken together, have been estimated at sixty billion tons—or about twenty tons of explosive for every inhabitant of the globe.[2]

It is difficult to grasp the meaning of such figures except by translating them into some tangible reality. For example, if the explosive power of a World War II blockbuster is represented by a one-foot ruler, the bomb that destroyed Hiroshima would be represented by the height of the Empire State Building, and the power of a twenty-megaton weapon by the height of the orbit of Sputnik I. "One thermonuclear bomb releases more destructive energy than that released by all of the bombs dropped on Germany and Japan during World War II."[3]

To give some notion of what such weapons could do:

A 20-megaton bomb exploded on the surface in the center of a town would blast a hole a mile across and eight hundred feet deep (about the height of the RCA Building in Rockefeller Center); the diameter of its fireball would be four and a half miles, and the blast would level everything over an area of about two hundred square miles (if the area were square, it would be about fourteen miles on a side); a deadly concentration of radioactive fallout would be showered over five thousand square miles—a square about seventy miles on a side.[4]

To speak of a nuclear war is to speak of a situation where such calamities as are described in the preceding citation would be multiplied dozens, and perhaps hundreds, of times across the continents of Europe and North America. The probable result, in the words of Bert Cochran, is that the belligerent countries "would be reduced to polluted junkheaps"[5]; and from what we know of the Hiroshima victims,[6] it is difficult not to believe that "the survivors would envy the dead."

Thus the kind of war that the use of nuclear weapons would surely produce makes it hard to draw any other conclusion than that the use of such weapons, under *any* circumstances, would be a moral atrocity so colossal as to be, quite literally, "beyond words." Attention to the problems entailed by the indefinitely continued possession and/or the use of these weapons leads, I believe, to the conclusion that they are by their very nature instruments of genocide, and that any foreign policy is morally irresponsible that does not explicitly aim at their abolition as soon as possible from the international scene.

In a sense, the bomb that exploded over the sands of New Mexico divided human history in two. The new age, which might well be called the age of Omnipotence,[7] has radically altered our relationship to ourselves and to the cosmos, confronting us with new realities, new problems, and new opportunities for which the guidelines are still indefinite. It demands new definitions of human reality, new procedures, new values, new kinds of loyalty. Failure to make the required adjustment cannot, in the end, be other than fatal. We must not permit ourselves the proud luxury of falling so in love with our technical ingenuity as to suppose that we can do absolutely anything we choose to do and get away with it, or that, in the words of Nat Hentoff, "we cannot become the first star to have willfully destroyed itself."

Yet it hardly need be said that such reconstructions of awareness are more readily called for than achieved. In the structure of human responsiveness, there are built-in sources of inertia that function as obstacles to the adjustment of perception to new realities; and this is more than ever true when the new realities are radically discontinuous with everything encountered heretofore. Human beings, like all creatures, function very largely by habit. This is normal and essential. We should no doubt become paralyzed if we had to decide consciously how to meet every new situation; hence, in the course of living we develop general patterns of more or less automatic response which "plug in" on the continuities of life, thus conserving the energy required for the making of higher-level (more complex) decisions, where the continuities are tenuous or nonexistent.

Such consistency of response is beneficial only so long as the major continuities persist. When they do not—when a radically new "situation" occurs—a major internal readjustment is demanded; we have to learn to see reality in quite new ways. Such readjustments are often painful; hence there is a tendency to seek to minimize anxiety by making new problems look like old ones and coping with them in the old ways. Such efforts tend to be less than satisfactory.

In the present case the possession by man of what could be called "absolute power" has radically altered the human situation; yet because of the inertia just now referred to, we have been trying to cope with this situation largely by means of conceptions and procedures native to the former "dispensation." These conceptions and procedures tend to treat the realities of the nuclear age as if nothing in the world had changed since 1945. This is particularly noticeable in the tendency in some quarters to discuss thermonuclear warfare as if it were simply a slightly beefed up version of conventional warfare (forgetting the near apocalyptic horrors that even conventional warfare has involved during the past three decades), in which one could still speak meaningfully of "shelters," "national aims," "victory," "national recovery," and the like. Such conceptual obsolescence entails human consequences of potentially catastrophic magnitude.

The tendency to deal with new realities by means of old definitions is a problem having to do in large measure with the limits of imagination. These limits are aggravated more than a little by the very magnitude of the discontinuity between the new realities and the old. The reality of any possible nuclear war is so apocalyptic—so vastly beyond the range of ordinary, normal experience—that we quite literally cannot believe in its reality in any truly existential sense. We "know," but we cannot "believe." [8] Most of us live in a cosmos that is more or less orderly and manageable; for the most part its constituting events fall within a certain limited compass. They are, in other words, more or less congruent with our own "size." For most of us, events of apocalyptic magnitude (on the order of a thermonuclear exchange) have never occurred; they have no real place in the cosmos that we inhabit. Such events, for us, possess no psychic reality; we may speak of them conceptually, in the context of strategy, politics, or technology, but we do not actually believe in them existentially. Even the fear they occasion is less fear than a kind of nagging, subliminal anxiety. Thus, thermonuclear war has become, in many respects, a concept without existential reality. Its increasingly apocalyptic dimensions have rendered it, ironically, not harder but easier to contemplate, with the passage of time—and therefore, by extension, easier to accept as a policy option. Scholars and military men, in the abstracted atmosphere of government-sponsored think tanks, discuss the strategies for a possible nuclear war, either as if they were discussing a catastrophe on Mars or as if the reality they referred to were merely a rather more stringent example of the kind of war that we have had in the past. Such discussions, by shielding us from the truly apocalyptic nature of the realities we contemplate, tend to seal us into a context of systematic illusion.

I began this chapter by suggesting that the ultimate challenge to modern man is whether we shall or shall not survive as a species, and that this challenge derives directly from our possession of apocalyptic power, notably in the form of thermonuclear weapons. This challenge is immensely complicated, as we are beginning to see, by the fact that the structure of thinking and feeling which is brought to bear on the problem of nuclear weapons, and of mass-destruction weapons generally, has itself been radically altered by them. The continuing existence of such weapons in the environment and their use as an instrument of policy among nations have exerted a profound impact on our sensitivities. To explore this impact in its various facets is the purpose of the chapters that follow.

## 2.

## REFLECTIONS
## FOR AN AGE OF OMNIPOTENCE

IN THE ANCIENT LITERATURE OF THE RACE THERE ARE NU-
merous fables and myths that touch in one fashion or
another upon the human drive toward power, mastery,
and control, together with the ambiguities that this drive
entails. One of these, of pagan origin, is the story of the
Sorcerer's Apprentice, in which the as-yet-unskilled novice
in the absence of his employer allows himself to suppose
that he is more clever than he really is. He proceeds by
magic to conjure up forces of nature and discovers to his
dismay that he cannot control them or turn them off. Order
is restored only by the return of the Sorcerer himself.

Another body of myth is found in the early chapters of
Genesis, where man, seeking to make himself the lord
and master of all creation, is first driven from the Garden
of Eden (the state of primal innocence and harmony) and
later foiled, through having his speech confused, in his
very attempt to storm the ramparts of heaven itself.

As stories of this type demonstrate, the dream of power
is very old—perhaps as old as the human race. It is found
in ancient cultures, where man devises methods by which
he bends the forces of nature to his own will, either by
compulsion (as in magic) or by persuasion (as in religion).

It is found also, and most notably, in the actual control that man exercises over the natural world through science and technology. The use of fire, the bow and arrow, the pulley, gunpowder, steam, the internal combustion engine, electricity, and finally atomic and nuclear power—all these testify to man's unquenchable thirst to bend the forces of nature to his own purposes, and his incredible success at doing so.

And yet, as the ancient myths all seem to suggest, this control involves a terrible ambiguity which man, in his pride, often fails to perceive. First, as implied in the story of the Apprentice, the natural forces that man builds into his machines do not "belong" to him. He himself did not create them. They already existed in the world; he merely discovered them and learned to harness them for his own ends. Thus, in the story, the powers that have been conjured into activity belong to the Sorcerer (God, Nature, or whatever is thought to be the ultimate ground of existence), not to the Apprentice. *He* merely uses them. Thus, man's first act of pride is the assumption that the forces of nature are his to do with as he pleases. Clearly they are not.

Moreover, as the same story suggests, the forces that man puts to work have a kind of independent existence. They are not entirely at his disposal. They exist in the world, whether or not man puts them to use. Once activated, they have a momentum of their own. Man has to start them; he also has to guide and terminate them, else they tend to run wild. Thus, "control" means not only the ability to activate natural powers otherwise only quiescent; it means also the ability to exercise responsible guidance over those powers once they are in motion, and to terminate them once their objectives have been achieved.

Another point to the story is that the natural forces, once

out of control, do not merely go off on their own; they turn around and attack the Apprentice. We sense a kind of ironic justice in this—partly because we recognize, if only subliminally, that the natural forces which the Apprentice puts into operation have no independent malice of their own; the malice they display is the malice that man himself puts into them via the purposes he builds into his machines.

> In fables of this kind, our sense of irony requires that the magic tool or machine which gets out of hand should not merely pursue an independent course unforeseen by the magician, but turn pointedly against him and defeat him. It is this irony, like the tragic irony in myths, which reveals to us that the independent malice the machine seems to bring to bear against us is in fact a reflexion of the destructive wish we unconsciously embodied in creating the machine.[1]

Thus, the machine, simple or complex, is an extension of ourselves. We build it, and we build into it the purposes that are already present in *us*. The powers of the machine are not our own, but the purposes and the objectives are. Accordingly the machine, whether it enriches or destroys us, is only turning upon us the results of our own decisions and the values they embody.

Turning to the Genesis mythology, we find recognized a similar kind of ambiguity. It is pictured first in the divine injunction to man: "Be fruitful and multiply, fill the earth and subdue it, rule over the fish in the sea, the birds of heaven, and every living thing that moves upon the earth" (Gen., ch. 1). The central image in this passage is clearly one of dominance, mastery, and control. Man is pictured as taking possession of and ruling over the various orders of nature. The power of this image derives from its accuracy;

it is simply a reflection of man's true being. In a certain sense, man *is* the ruler of nature. Of all the forms of life, he alone has the ability, in more than superficial ways, to modify the shape of reality by injecting into it his own "image" and purposes. He alone is able to rearrange the materials of life, to create new modes of existence.

And yet the Biblical image also reflects the understanding that man's capacity for dominance is one that fills his life with ambiguities, not the least of which is the almost continual temptation to the sin of pride. For through pride man tends to exercise his dominance as if he were free of all restraints—as if he were answerable to no one or nothing beyond his own will. Through pride he tends to want to believe that he has escaped the logic, the laws, and the limitations of the natural order. Through pride he tends to picture himself as the lord and master of all things, able to "run the universe," and to do so according to his own specifications.

But man, the Genesis mythology tells us, cannot succeed in doing this. Life is not made that way. There is something in the nature of things that stands over against him. This reality cannot be manipulated or disposed of. It carries an authority that is absolute. It tells him, in a general way, if he is not too stupid and arrogant to pay heed, what he may do and what he may not do if he wants to gain the fullness of life. In the Biblical tradition this reality is called "God," and the affirmation is made again and again that man cannot gain the fullness of life unless he exercises his capacity for dominance and control in accordance with God's will.[2] In the Biblical understanding, prideful disobedience to God's will brings punishment. In the Garden of Eden myth, man seeks to become God's equal (that is, he seeks to appropriate all power by becoming equal to the

Source of all power), and is driven from the garden. Later, he seeks to build a tower that will reach up to heaven (that is, he attempts to occupy the seat of all authority), and is foiled in his attempt by having his speech confused (that is, even such power and authority as he has are fragmented and thereby reduced). In myths of this type the common theme is clear: When man, through pride, allows himself to imagine that his lordship over creation has in some fashion exempted him from the limitations of finitude, he is brought low, and his pride is chastised.

The control that is given sanction in the Genesis mythology is *responsible* control. Responsible control means the use of power in ways that reverence the sanctity of human life and the integrity of creation as a whole. Irresponsible control—the use of power capriciously, wantonly, and exploitively in the spirit of prideful self-assertion or for essentially destructive purposes—entails consequences that may be thought of as a form of judgment.

The history of civilization, from one perspective, is the history of technology. It is the history of man's persistent self-extension, through appropriation of the forces of nature, and their increasingly sophisticated application as instruments of control, whereby the shape of the environment and the shape of human life itself are determined in accordance with human purposes, both good and evil. From this perspective, technology expresses the essence of man. Other animals adjust themselves (as they can) to fit the environment as given; man re-creates the environment to fit himself. Thus, the world man lives in is largely an artifact—an extension of his own being.

In the course of history, this extension of self, this appropriation of power, has escalated beyond all bounds. The process that began with the hand ax has finally culminated in that most remarkable and problematic of all conjurings whereby the genius of man summoned forth the power of the suns from the recesses of the universe. In this respect, one might say, we have become "as Gods": we have gathered unto ourselves more power than we at one time attributed to our deities. The gods of the ancient world did not surpass the magnitude of sheer physical force that has fallen into our hands. The fate of Sodom and Gomorrah has been repeated already several times through the agency of modern man, and the cataclysmic predictions of John's Revelation hardly surpass in sheer magnitude the apocalypse now made possible by the products of human technology.

The magnitude of power now appropriated by the relentless technological genius of man dramatizes more starkly than ever before the terrible ambiguity attendant upon man's lordship of the planet. No other factor so directly confronts man with his own potentialities for good or evil. The limits in both directions have been extended almost without measure. We have the power, at this juncture, to create goodness previously undreamed of; we are also able, using the same power, to create an equally unimagined evil. Both the good and the evil are potentially without limit. We could, if we chose, create conditions for "a new heaven and a new earth"; we could, at the other extreme, lay waste the planet in a spasm of literally total destruction. Where the alternatives are potentially so consequential, the demand for responsible stewardship of power assumes a vastly expanded significance. We are, indeed, masters of the planet. In our hands is the power of life and death—not only for some but for all. This power is now part of our very being; it cannot be lost. Thus we cannot escape the consequences of our acts, for we ourselves are part of the total fabric of life which our acts will either enhance or destroy. The brotherhood of life imposes itself upon us, and the reality of Judgment cannot be escaped.

Technology, then, may be seen as problematic in that it magnifies the human capacity both for good and for evil; it does this by making more and more of the forces of nature available to human control. These forces in themselves are ethically neutral; they lend themselves equally to all purposes, regardless of moral content. Their essential effect is to expand the capacity of those who appropriate them to achieve their aims, whatever those aims may be.[3]

If the forces of nature are ethically neutral, the aims of men are never so. Certainly the history of technology raises a serious question concerning the supposed "neutrality" of science. Why have the purposes of man, as embodied in the machine, been so preponderately on the side of malevolence? Why has the self-extension of man, the drive to control the powers of nature, expressed itself through such a disproportionately great fascination with implements of destruction?

In his play *Man and Superman,* George Bernard Shaw puts into the mouth of the Devil (!) the following wry discourse:

> Have you walked up and down the earth lately? I have; and I have examined man's wonderful inventions. And I tell you that in the arts of life man invents nothing, but in the arts of death he outdoes nature herself, and produces by chemistry and machinery all the slaughter of plague, pestilence, and famine. The peasant I tempt today eats and drinks what was eaten and drunk by peasants of ten thousand years ago; and the house he lives in has not altered as much in a thousand centuries as the fashion of a lady's

bonnet in a score of weeks. But when he goes out to slay, he carries a marvel of mechanism that lets loose at the touch of his finger all the hidden molecular energies, and leaves the javelin, the arrow, the blow-pipe of his fathers far behind.[4]

The statement is exaggerated, but not without point. War taxes, as William James observed, are the only ones men never hesitate to pay,[5] and war technology, one might well add, is the one technology that consistently outstrips its competitors in the race for public acceptance and support.[6]

On the basis of his own researches, Lewis Mumford has concluded that weapons development is the basis not only of war technology but of nearly all technology. Industrial technology, he claims, did not develop under its own impetus; its major achievements came into being as by-products of weapons research.

[T]he partnership between the soldier, the miner, the technician, and the scientist is an ancient one. To look upon the horrors of modern warfare as the accidental result of fundamentally innocent and peaceful technical development is to forget the elementary facts of the machine's history.

. . . . The most important fact about modern warfare is the steady increase of mechanization from the fourteenth century onward: Here militarism forced the pace and cleared a straight path to the development of modern large scale standardized industry.[7]

Mumford's researches are too lengthy, of course, to repeat here. A few of his examples will suffice to illustrate his conclusion:

1. In France, he points out, the development of smelting was a product of military demand. "At the end of the

[sixteenth] century France had thirteen foundries, all devoted to the manufacture of canon—the only other important articles being scythes." [8]

2. "The gun was the starting point of a new type of power machine: it was, mechanically speaking, a one-cylinder internal combustion engine: the first form of the modern gasoline engine, and some of the early experiments in using explosive mixtures in motors sought to employ powder rather than a liquid fuel." [9]

3. The pressure of military demand, he notes, gave impetus to the organization of the factory, and to the development of standardization and mass production; these developments were due to the need for mass-produced hand weapons (e.g., muskets) with standardized interchangeable parts.[10]

4. Finally, the development of high-grade steel was a consequence of military demand. "Napoleon III in the middle of the nineteenth century offered a reward for a cheap process of making steel capable of withstanding the explosive force of the new shells. The bessemer process was the direct answer to this demand." [11]

One might also note that the continuing technical improvements of the airplane have occurred largely under military pressure. Generally speaking, most new aircraft are developed for military purposes and later adapted to civilian use—or, if developed under nonmilitary auspices, their military possibilities are quickly noted and seized upon.

The same is true in medicine, where much of the progress takes place under the pressure of wartime needs. It would seem that only under such conditions is the sense of urgency sufficiently high to sustain intensive research. (It should also be noted, surely, that wartime medicine is not developed for essentially "humane" reasons; its primary objective is to get wounded soldiers back into battle as quickly as possible.)

Finally, it is worth noting that the very first use of atomic energy was military. Except for the pressure of wartime necessity (i.e., to beat Hitler to the punch), it is likely that atomic energy would not have been effectively harnessed for several years following the date on which it actually was harnessed. Thus, again, the question: Why is the power to destroy so much more able than other forms of power to enlist the commitment and the ingenuity of man?

There is no way to answer this question with any certainty. Yet the way to an answer may be found by considering the ultimate meaning of power as an attribute of the human sense of self. At its most basic level, power has to do with our very existence as persons. Even merely to exist is to assert oneself against the power of nonbeing—to stand against all that limits, obstructs, or destroys the self. Yet beyond mere existence, we affirm ourselves by seeking in some fashion to impress the shape of our lives upon the world around us. We endeavor to change something—to make the world at least in some small way different by virtue of our existence. (This is one reason why people have children—or write books!) By doing this, we affirm to the world and to ourselves, "I exist; my life is proven to have substance." This is an assertion of power.

At social levels we assert our existence and worth by impressing ourselves upon the lives of other persons. In this context, power means having the kind of impact on others that leads them to recognize and affirm our being. Such power is extremely crucial to our existence. Without it, we could not survive, not even physically. We all need to be affirmed by others, and without this affirmation by others no self-affirmation is even possible. People learn from others whether or not their lives have worth and value. (To have worth and value is to have power; as we say, "to *be* something.") There is no other way for this to happen. Research has shown that babies who are not loved (i.e., not affirmed as having worth and value) may become insane or may actually die.

Power is often thought of as a necessary evil at best. One thinks of Lord Acton's famous dictum: "Power tends to corrupt, and absolute power corrupts absolutely." This is misleading, for without power there is no self. Even to *be* a self is to share to some extent in the power of being.

Thus it is a mistake to say that power corrupts. On the contrary, it is weakness that corrupts. It is the silent knowledge of our weakness that instills in us the lust for power in the form of dominion, that makes us want to banish our limitations by the exercise of mastery. In our weakness we seek to enhance the self by lording it over anything that potentially reminds us of our limits: the powers of nature, the powers of other men.

There is something of this lust in all of us. For, in the last analysis, we are *all* weak: we are finite, limited. Our lives are fragile: the forces that sustain us can also destroy us at a moment's notice, and eventually they always do—every self-assertion is merely a postponement of the final descent into nonbeing. Our lives, in the last analysis, are not at our disposal.

Thus there is in all men the hidden temptation to pride, a hatred for their own limitedness, a wish to deny or destroy anything that escapes their control. And even to those who understand the implications and the dangers of their own finitude, there are deep satisfactions in the exercise of dominion.

There is no clearer symbol of dominion than the weapon. In all technology there is promise of dominion: by technology man is able to alter the shape of reality, to impress his own "image" upon the rest of life, to make himself master of the forces of nature and the destinies of other men. Yet, in the weapon, this promise of dominion is carried to its ultimate point: the power to destroy. The power to destroy is the final form of self-assertion. It is the power to cancel what other men, by *their* power, have produced—the power, indeed, to take from other men the very power even to *be*. The striving for such power is a quest for the illusion of omnipotence—whereby men strive to banish the knowledge of their own finitude.

It is surely ironic, therefore, that the quest for omnipotence only succeeds in strengthening the limitations of finitude by making life even more fragile and dangerous than before. This is so because the appropriation of greater levels of killing power over others is always matched by the appropriation of more or less equivalent levels of killing power by those "others" against oneself. For the ordinary citizen, of course, the power equation is quite asymmetrical: he experiences only the fragility. Since most people do not have access to nuclear bombs, the satisfactions of power for them are strictly the vicarious ones of imagining what "we" could do to "them" if they get too uppity. (In this case, "we" is really a form of "they": those who, in our behalf—though not necessarily with our consent—man the nuclear barricades.) Hence, for most people, "omnipotence" means only the omnipotence of what can be done *to* them by *others:* i.e., nuclear incineration. This awareness doubtless reinforces the often in-articulate sense people have (1) that their lives are at the mercy of remote, and essentially malevolent, power structures ("they"), or (2) that mankind as a whole is caught helplessly in the grip of runaway technical or historical forces which transcend human control.

Men confronted by such a situation suspect, understandably, that they are caught in a kind of trap. This is so because a quest that seeks an objective that cannot be attained is a quest without an end point. Thus the attempt to banish finitude by the appropriation of destructive power is an enterprise doomed to "succeed" only by a process of endless escalation.

Now that man's appropriation of destructive power has approached a kind of totality, the warning of the Sorcerer's Apprentice comes back to haunt us. We have managed to get the genie out of the bottle; the overriding question is: Can we get it back in again? This question dramatizes the terrible paradox faced by those who appropriate the upper limits of power. Possession of power means control—control over nature, control over other men. Yet power of this magnitude, when gathered into such frail vessels as man is able to assemble, threatens continually to escape and run wild, thereby nullifying the control that its possession originally promised, as well as possibly destroying the possessor besides. Are we not, in a sense, at the mercy of our machines—at the mercy, indeed, of our own demonic ingenuity?

The question is crucial, because the issue of the nuclear weapon is the issue of control—not control over nature and society which the weapon symbolizes, but control of the weapon itself.[12] On this issue hangs the life—or death—of mankind.

# 3.
## DETERRENCE:
## THE DEADLY PARADOX

SINCE 1945, THE EXISTENCE OF WEAPONS OF POTENTIALLY unlimited destructiveness has forced into the consciousness of nations the concept of weapons as instruments essentially for preventing rather than waging or winning of war. The very magnitude of existing nuclear weapons threatens, in their prospective use, a destruction so massive as to be unbearable. Hence their possession by the great powers is assumed to impose upon them a deterrent factor of extremely high efficacy: each side is "deterred" from using its own nuclear arsenal, or from otherwise grossly overstepping the boundaries of acceptable international behavior, by the prospect of drawing upon itself a retaliatory strike of potentially unlimited devastation. Thus, in essence, the purpose of deterrent policy is, by *threatening* destruction, to *avoid* the necessity of imposing it. In other words, to reduce, to the zero point if possible, the likelihood of a general war by making general war too horrendous to be acceptable as a live option to either side.

Deterrence is by no means a new concept. All weapons contain a deterrence factor, since their possession threatens potential enemies with unwanted damage in the event of aggression. But deterrence has never in the past functioned with more than a limited efficacy. When the desired political objectives to be achieved from the initiation of armed conflict are accorded greater weight than the undesired costs entailed by such conflict, deterrence no longer deters. Like the threat of police action in a society, its major function has been to increase the cost of unacceptable behavior and thus to raise the boundary above which such behavior is likely to be attempted.

Nuclear deterrence, however, imposes a new factor: it radically escalates the cost of misbehavior. Both sides recognize that the massive destruction of their society is a consequence in which any conceivable objectives would simply be swallowed up. In this sense, nuclear deterrence "works": it motivates both sides to avoid initiating a major conflict that they recognize would destroy all the possible objectives in whose behalf such conflicts have traditionally been fought.

There has not been a general war since 1945. It is impossible to determine whether or not the policy of nuclear deterrence is solely responsible for this, since there is no way of empirically testing past events, yet it is possible that the inescapable danger of nuclear exchange contained in any direct military confrontation has caused the United States and Russia to avoid such confrontations. If so, the effect of nuclear deterrence has been to drive the conflict down to lower levels, where the danger of a nuclear response is less serious.

"Deterrence strategies," as Jerome Frank observes, "are intended to achieve a posture that without heightening international tension or provoking the adversary into further arming clearly signals determination to retaliate if he attacks." [1] The ideal deterrent, in other words, would find just that level of strength necessary to deter but not to provoke. It would be such as to indicate certain retaliation in the event of attack, but *only* in the event of attack. Needless to say, such an ideal deterrent has not been found. Even the best deterrent strategy available, within the boundaries of current imagination, contains built-in flaws which erode its viability as a permanent policy. Nuclear deterrence "works" in the short run, but I believe there is some question as to whether it will do so in the long run.

The major limitation of all deterrence systems, nuclear or otherwise, is their tendency to deter and to provoke at the same time. They achieve their objectives by promoting on each side an awareness of itself as being threatened by the other. All such threats, explicit or implicit, promote a certain element of mutual mistrust. Each side is conscious of itself as targeted by the other's weapons, and neither side can ever be entirely certain what the other side will or will not do with those weapons. Thus the appeal of deterrence essentially is to fear, and through fear, to hostility. Deterrence requires for its successful functioning mutual perceptions that maintain bad relations and undercut the search for accommodation. Continuing bad relations, in turn, perpetuate the need to maintain the deterrent, thus leading to a self-reinforcing spiral. Continuing bad relations perpetuate the possibility of crisis, in which the danger of escalation is always present.

Thus there is a degree of instability in all deterrence systems. This instability is complicated by further instabilities inherent in the nature of modern technology. Weapons technology, like all modern technology, is itself unstable: it develops at an extremely rapid pace. Therefore the stalemate on which successful deterrence depends is always in danger of being upset. The fear that prevents each protagonist from initiating hostilities *also* impels him to reduce the threat to his own society by seeking to develop a deterrent of his own that will nullify that of his adversary. Each side, in the interest of its own security, must seek to make itself significantly less vulnerable than the other. Yet the very achievement of such an objective—actual or seeming—would be self-defeating, for it would substantially increase on both sides the pressure toward the *use* of the weapons hitherto deployed only for deterrence. The temporarily disadvantaged nation, in self-defense, would be tempted to strike before the first nation could exploit its advantage; the nation that made the breakthrough, seeing its temporary advantage, would be tempted to strike while that advantage was still its, or more probably because it feared that the other nation might strike in the fear that *it* would do so.[2]

Any human dynamic based on fear contains an element of paradox. Even as it "works," elements within it tend to sabotage its full success. Thus the effect of the nuclear deterrent has been, so far, to forestall direct U.S.-Soviet military confrontations, in the interest of more indirect, circumscribed methods of conflict. Yet the dangers of such conflict are enhanced by the continual temptation to persist more stubbornly in the pursuit of one's objectives, using the nuclear threat as a source of pressure toward their attainment. Thus, as John Bennett observes, it is often assumed

> that if we are resolute enough to make our deterrent credible, the other side will always yield. Much of the willingness to defend the use of nuclear weapons is based upon the assumption that if the people on our side show enough toughness, enough readiness to use them, they never will have to be used.[3]

Interestingly, this assumption works—at least it has worked so far (since we are still here). Yet the game is extremely dangerous, because it is a game that both sides can play. If "we" persist, in the assumption that "they" will yield, and if "they" persist, in the assumption that "we" will yield, the game can have only one possible conclusion. Thus the dynamic of this game is to invest even limited objectives with potentially unlimited consequences. Every confrontation becomes, potentially, a nuclear confrontation.

Moreover, success in playing this game could multiply the dangers inherent in it. It could lead to arrogance and recklessness. It could be resorted to with increasing readiness, in the interest of ever more limited objectives. Such recklessness is clearly the very opposite of the type of response that deterrence strategies intend.

Thus it is clear that while all forms of deterrence are to some degree paradoxical, nuclear deterrence, by its own special nature, is paradoxical in a fashion peculiar to itself. This paradox is derived from the potentially "absolute" nature of the weapons involved. Its effect is to introduce a grotesque disproportion between any possible objectives that might be sought or defended and the price that their attainment might require.[4] To limited political objectives (and all political objectives are limited) is attached a price tag that is potentially *un*limited. The price tag itself is paradoxical: to *avoid* paying it, we must be *willing* to pay it; and if we do end up having to pay it, we have thereby canceled completely the objective on whose behalf it was paid.

Putting it another way: nuclear weapons, by their very dreadfulness, act as a powerful deterrent against major war; yet their very existence makes major war possible, and the dreadfulness which deters also insures that, if it comes, war will be that much worse than it otherwise would have been. Nuclear weapons, as a deterrent, function to preserve civilization from the scourge of a major conflict; yet if deterrence fails and the nuclear weapons are used, "they will destroy all that their possession is intended to defend." [5] Thus the very instruments through which war is prevented would serve to make war, if it comes, so terrible as, in retrospect, to nullify the justice of the policy which, by seeking (unsuccessfully) to prevent it, had actually brought it about.

The paradox defined here may be translated into the language of social and political options by means of such questions as the following:

1. Is it right to defend valid social values by means of a policy which, if unsuccessful, is likely to destroy those values even more completely than they would have been destroyed with no defense at all?

2. Is it right to choose a policy involving (for the time being) a low risk of unlimited evil, as opposed to a policy involving the high risk of lesser evils?

3. Is it right to preserve *limited* values by incurring the risk of *unlimited* cost—especially when the cost must be carried by millions of people who have not been consulted about the choice?

4. Is it right, for the sake of its short-run benefits (if they *are* benefits), to pursue a policy that is likely to be *unsuccessful* in the long run—especially when there is no way of knowing just how long, or how short, that "long run" will be?

Questions of this kind expose rather concretely the moral paradox implicit in all nuclear deterrence strategies. It is a paradox because it links together two contradictory conditions: deterrence appears to be a genuinely moral option as long as it works; yet it can be said truly to work only if it works *perfectly*—only, that is, *if it never breaks down*. But that judgment can never be rendered, for the working of deterrence is always strictly a *past* event—there is no way of knowing whether, or how long, it will continue to work in the future. And its failure to work at some future date would, by destroying even more completely all that it had sought to defend, thereby have absolutely nullified any and all moral claims that it had made for itself up to that time.

The paradox of weapons whose *non*-use can be assured only by their readiness for *use* is ultimately a paradox of intention. Deterrence functions effectively only if we are able to communicate a willingness to *use* the weapons whose use deterrence is designed to *prevent*.[6] Thus, in order to prevent a war that both sides know is utterly disproportionate to any conceivable objective, we must be *willing*, if necessary, to launch such a war—and we must make certain that this willingness is well understood as an international fact. Such a stated willingness entails two serious consequences: (1) It establishes the possibility that such a war could actually occur—thereby tending to sabotage the very purpose (i.e., deterrence) of the willingness itself. (2) It establishes, in the words of James Douglass, "an essential conflict between the apparently moral acts of deterring or limiting warfare and their fundamentally immoral means in the nuclear age: the intention to wage thermonuclear genocide." [7] Or, to put it more simply: an apparently moral act (deterrence) seems to require for its successful operation the maintenance and the vigorous proclamation of a grossly immoral intention (the intention, if necessary, to wage thermonuclear genocide).

I fail to see how the maintenance and the proclamation, by national states over a long period of time, of a grossly immoral intention can have any other effect than the morally corrupting one of enhancing the generally perceived legitimacy of such intentions as a normal dimension of policy. This, in fact, is precisely what has taken place. Thus, in the long run, the logic of nuclear deterrence has been to contribute to the spread of moral sensitivities that perceive the willing—and, by extension, the doing—of genocide as morally acceptable.

# 4.
# ESCALATING
## THE ACCEPTABLE

RAYMOND AARON HAS CALLED THE PRESENT AGE "THE CEN-
tury of total war." This is no idle rhetoric: the present
century has distinguished itself, by comparison with its
predecessors, chiefly by the ingenuity and thoroughness
with which its inhabitants have learned to dispose of each
other whenever it is seen as politically advantageous to do
so. This is not because twentieth-century men are innately
more bloodthirsty or barbaric than their forebears; it is simply because they have at their disposal an array of killing-
machines much more efficient and powerful than those of
any past generation. In this century we have done more
grotesquely horrendous things than have ever been done
before. But we have not done them because we are
savages; we have done them simply because we *could*.

This is not to suggest that moral judgment has been
absent from our calculations. Quite the contrary, moral
judgment often has been present, but it has demonstrated
a tendency to accommodate itself to whatever level of
violence was currently extant before deciding what kind
and degree of violence was permissible. The "is" and the
"ought" have stayed rather close together. Thus, as in
recent history the level of armed violence either done or

planned has escalated, there has been a more or less corresponding escalation of the limits of violence judged to be
"morally acceptable." This escalation of judgment has in
turn given sanction to the further escalation of violence itself.

Clearly, moral perception is no independent variable.
We do not simply decide what is right and wrong from
a position, as it were, "above the battle"; the very modes of
perception that inform our judging have been largely ab-
sorbed at a prerational level and have been shaped by
events prior to any decision we ourselves have made. Thus
the logic, the quality, of moral perception is, to some degree, shaped by factors beyond our control, or even beyond
our recognition. We judge as we "see"; yet the "seeing"
itself is prior to our own decision.

The point here is that the quality of moral perception
can be altered, as it were, "behind our backs," by events
that are not recognized or admitted as part of the moral
equation. When this happens, there is a form of self-deception: we are unable to recognize that any change has taken
place. We may continue to verbalize previously functioning principles without recognizing that their meaning has
become radically distorted; or we may conveniently "forget" the position we formerly held. In the present context,
the dynamics by which this alteration of sensitivity occurs
may be defined by reference to three principles.

## I. The Self-reinforcing Character of Violence

The first principle is that violence itself, with or without
weapons of mass destruction, tends to be self-reinforcing.
Under the pressure of mounting hatred, the progressive
destruction of order, and the explicit or implicit removal

of traditional restraints, increasingly high levels of violence become emotionally and morally acceptable. Under such conditions men are rendered capable either of doing or of sanctioning brutalities that under more usual circumstances would repel them. Their responses to "the enemy" tend to become more massive and less discriminating. Discussion of ethics or policy tends to become propagandistic and crudely self-justifying. Thus, it is generally agreed, for example, that the obliteration bombing of German cities in World War II was undertaken partly in revenge for the German bombing of British and other cities.[1] A British spokesman formulated the government's policy in the following terms: "Our plans are to bomb, burn, and ruthlessly destroy in every possible way available to us the people responsible for creating this war."[2] This statement stands in marked contrast to the moderation characteristic of earlier pronouncements (see below, section II); its essentially indiscriminate hostility is revealed in its crude reference to *"the people"* responsible for creating the war—meaning, clearly, the entire German populace taken as a whole. Under the mentality engendered by immediately previous violence, the German people, taken as a whole, had become a single collective target against whom unlimited, indiscriminate violence was now permissible.

A similar trend is easily visible in the American war against Indochina. In the bombing of North Vietnam, June–July 1966, precautions were taken to ensure that the attacks would be precise, discriminate, and minimally damaging to civilian life.[3] But by 1968, according to some pilots, the whole of North Vietnam had become, in effect, a "free drop zone" in which "there were no forbidden targets."[4] Likewise, earlier pronouncements about defending the "freedom" of the people of Indochina later gave way to more tough-minded commentary, as, for example, the statement by an American diplomat: "In order to make progress in this country [Laos], it is necessary to level everything. It is necessary to reduce the inhabitants to zero." [5]

## II. The Self-legitimizing Character of the Existent (Habituation)

The second principle is that an existing situation, policy, or practice, long enough maintained, tends with the passage of time to be increasingly accepted as legitimate, regardless of its merits. Even a situation initially seen as repugnant cannot continue indefinitely to command the same intensity of response. We come gradually to accept it as a "given"; and what is accepted as "given" will in time be accepted as "legitimate." [6] Thus, by the process known as "habituation," an evil, once made acceptable, tends to become increasingly so; and the consequent erosion of moral inhibition makes possible an escalation of performance. One thinks of the lines from Alexander Pope: "Vice is a monster of so frightful mien,/As to be hated needs but to be seen;/Yet seen too oft, familiar with her face,/We first endure, then pity, then embrace."

The alteration of moral perception through habituation has been clearly operative in the development of mass destruction, and its general acceptance as a licit policy of warfare. The history of this development has been well documented; only a few of the highlights need to be mentioned here.

1. 1937. The town of Guernica is bombed; several hundred civilians killed. World response: moral outrage.

2. 1937. The Japanese bomb Nanking. The United States Government protests: "This Government holds the view that any general bombing of an extensive area wherein there resides a large populace engaged in peaceful pursuits is unwarranted and contrary to the principles of law and humanity." [7]

3. 1939. Nazi invasion of Poland; bombardment of Warsaw by the Luftwaffe; many civilians killed.

4. 1939. President Roosevelt publicly affirms that "the ruthless bombings from the air of civilians in unfortified centers of population . . . has profoundly shocked the conscience of humanity. . . . I am therefore addressing this urgent appeal to every government which may be engaged in hostilities publically to affirm its determination that its armed forces shall in no event, and in no circumstances, undertake the bombardment from the air of civilian populations or of unfortified cities." [8]

5. 1940. Bombing of Rotterdam by the Luftwaffe. Several hundred civilians killed.

6. 1940. Winston Churchill denounces the bombing of cities as "a new and odious form of attack." The Foreign Office affirms: "His Majesty's Government have made it clear that it is no part of their policy to bomb non-military objectives, no matter what the policy of the German Government may be. In spite of the wanton and repeated attacks of the German Air Force on undefended towns in Poland, Norway, France, Holland, and Belgium, His Majesty's Government steadily adhere to this policy." [9]

7. 1940. Luftwaffe initiates aerial warfare against London and other British cities.

8. 1940. R.A.F. commences air raids on German industrial cities.

9. 1942. Air Marshall Sir Arthur Travers Harris takes

over R.A.F.'s bomber command. Initiation of policy of "obliteration bombing," designed both to destroy industrial targets and to terrorize the German populace and cripple their "will to resist." Churchill—who two years previously has denounced the bombing of cities as an "odious form of attack"—now informs the House of Commons that Germany is to be subjected to "an ordeal, the like of which has never been experienced by any country." [10]

10. 1943. Churchill reaffirms the policy of obliteration bombing: "There are no sacrifices we will not make, no lengths of violence to which we will not go." [11]

11. 1943. The U.S. Eighth Air Force joins the R.A.F. in a daily schedule of obliteration bombing of German cities.

12. 1943. The bombing of Hamburg. Estimated death toll: 43,000 to 50,000. [12]

13. 1944. The bombing of Darmstadt. Estimated death toll: 12,000 to 15,000. [13]

14. 1945. The bombing of Dresden—a city crowded at the time with refugees, and containing no significant military targets. A "firestorm" was deliberately created, in which an estimated 135,000 people perished. [14]

15. 1945. The United States begins fire-bomb raids on Japanese cities. Estimated death toll in Tokyo raid: 100,000. [15]

This catalog of events illustrates how easily moral perception can be altered by the impact of external events, and how quickly acts once judged abhorrent can be made to seem not only acceptable but laudable. Those who affirm that man is an essentially rational being in control of his actions should consider the implications of the foregoing. In this case, a radical change in moral sensitivity took place. At each point in the sequence, men were "in control" of their actions: they were doing what they "willed" to do.

Yet their will had *itself* been altered, without their previous "consent" or recognition, by forces beyond their control.

A major casualty in the shift was the integrity of moral conscience, including Christian conscience, and the erosion of serious commitment to the traditional principles of discrimination and proportionality as limiting criteria in the conduct and assessment of morally justifiable warfare. For instance, a report issued in 1944 by the Federal Council of Churches Commission on the Relation of the Church to the War in the Light of Christian Faith, while condemning "the massacre of civilian populations" as morally unjustifiable, nevertheless went on to state that

> some of the signers of the report believe that certain other measures, such as rigorous blockades of foodstuffs essential to civilian life, and obliteration bombing of civilian areas, however repugnant to humane feelings, are still justifiable on Christian principles, if they are essential to the successful conduct of a war that is itself justified.[16]

From the standpoint of conscience, Christian or otherwise, such a statement represents an outrageous equivocation. Thus it is not surprising to discover an eminent churchman stating wryly, in the context of another Commission:

> The norm of practically effective inhibitions turns out to be, after all, military decisiveness; and beyond ruling out wanton destructiveness [?], Christian conscience in wartime seems to have chiefly the effect . . . of making Christians do reluctantly what military necessity requires.[17]

"What military necessity requires" had, in the progress of World War II, dragged the moral conscience of humanity down ever more deeply into the mire of a new barbarism.

Supposed "military necessity" led the way; ethics followed behind, faintly protesting but nonetheless keeping within hailing distance. "And so it was," as Robert Batchelder writes,

> that within seven years a radical change in military practice and moral judgements had taken place. What was universally condemned by churchmen and decent people generally in 1937, and considered fit only for dictators in 1939, was between 1940 and 1944 accepted as a "military necessity" and a normal part of the procedure of war, both by the general public and by the large majority of churchmen, both Protestant and Catholic.[18]

There can be no doubt that the habituation of the human conscience, during the course of World War II, to the routine practice of massive indiscriminate destruction of enemy populations was a major factor leading to the acceptance of the atomic bomb as a licit instrument of total warfare against cities. In a brilliant article written in 1944 protesting the policy of obliteration bombing, Fr. John C. Ford, a Jesuit moralist, issued this warning in clear terms:

> Even if obliteration bombing did shorten the war . . . and even if it did save military lives, we still must consider what the result for the future will be if this means of warfare is made generally legitimate.
> . . . . The recognition of obliteration bombing will easily and quickly lead to the recognition of total war itself. . . . Obliteration bombing has taken us a long step in the direction of immoral total war. To justify it will, I believe, make it exceedingly difficult to draw the line at further barbarities in practice.[19]

Robert Batchelder has analyzed in some detail the events leading to the decision to drop the bomb on Hiroshima and Nagasaki. Though other options were reviewed, he says, none save the use of the bomb on cities was considered seriously. This was not because the men responsible for making this decision were barbarians: the very structure of their thinking on the matter had already been preconditioned by a three-year policy in which unlimited, indiscriminate violence had become fully routinized. As Batchelder points out:

> By July 1945, when targets for the atomic bomb were chosen, the word target had come to be synonymous with the word city, so far as Japan was concerned. The loss of the distinction between military targets and urban areas can be seen clearly in the accounts of those who chose the atomic bomb targets. The choice of cities as targets for the atomic bomb was unquestioned and automatic.[20]

With such a legacy behind us, it is not surprising that the way was made open thereafter for ever more and more powerful and destructive bombs, whose use as instruments of total war was dictated by their very magnitude. No significant restraints were operative save the technical limitations on what could actually be produced. Thus it was not long before the atomic bomb was rendered obsolete by the development of the nuclear bomb—one thousand times as powerful as its predecessor. The mere existence of such a weapon on the world scene had a serious impact on human sensitivities. We learned increasingly to perceive apocalyptic degrees of destructive power as "ordinary" and "routine," and in so doing, accommodated ourselves progressively to the notion that some form of "limited" nuclear war might be a viable enterprise after all.

This development can best be appreciated by contrast with the perceptions which it so swiftly replaced. The initial ideology of the atomic age saw the Bomb (even a bomb of "only" twenty kilotons) as the absolute weapon: its use as a means of unlimited mass destruction against a total society was accepted as being implicit in its very magnitude. This assumption was greeted with a kind of desperate hopefulness. The "absolute" weapon, it was thought, would serve as an "absolute" deterrent. War, henceforth, would become so terrible that it could never again be seriously considered as a live option by reasonable men. Between the great powers, at least, the certainty of unbearable mutual devastation would compel a result that nothing else had hitherto been able to achieve: the abolition of war as an instrument of national policy.

These notions, of course, did not survive long: it should have been recognized at the very outset that there is nothing so "terrible" that it cannot be considered as a live option by men, reasonable or otherwise. By the early 1950's the ideology of the "absolute" weapon was being systematically questioned by strategists in the interest of more traditional military doctrines. What had seemed "absolute" in 1945 did not seem quite so "absolute" seven or eight years later. Since it was increasingly recognized that nuclear war might occur despite efforts to prevent it, much thought was thenceforth devoted to the proposition that, should such a war come, we should be prepared to "win" it.

Clearly, a war that can be "won" is a "limited" war—by definition (at least for the winning side): if you still exist after the war is over, there is some sense in which that war was less than "absolute." This notion captured the imagination of the strategists, and thenceforth we became committed to the doctrine of "limited" nuclear war. "The problem today is limited war. . . . Since nuclear war may be a necessity, it must be made a possibility. Its possibility must be created." [21]

The doctrine of limited nuclear war is the doctrine that nuclear weapons—even megaton weapons—are *not* intrinsically weapons of total annihilation. Like "conventional" weapons, they can and should be used discriminately. Specifically, the doctrine of limited war is the doctrine that nuclear war can be conducted rationally and morally, by using one's weaponry in a counterforce capacity—that is, against military instead of civilian targets.[22] Thus, "limited" nuclear war is not limited in scope or destructiveness; it is still a war of megaton proportions. It is still a war that, by the estimates of its proponents, would measure the dead by the dozens of millions. Its "limitations" are connected solely with the matter of "discriminate aiming." Accordingly, when the nuclear strategists speak of "limited war," the "limits" they refer to have little to do with the magnitude of destruction, only with the aiming process that leads to it.

It is tragic to see how readily otherwise valid moral criteria for the restraint of organized violence have been subverted by long exposure to the prospect of a technicized apocalypse into serving as the rationale for what by most traditional standards of judgment is nothing less than wholesale slaughter. The moral claim for a counterforce nuclear strategy is grounded in the principle of discrimination: it is counter-*force*, not counter-*society*. Its targets are (supposedly) specific, not general. Yet megaton weapons, and in most cases even kiloton weapons, by their very magnitude are inherently indiscriminate. They are "area" weapons: the scope of destruction that they inflict reduces the matter of "discriminate aiming" to a moral sophistry.

In all highly industrialized societies, military and civilian centers are contiguous. Even "justly targeted" nuclear weapons could scarcely destroy the one without destroying the other just as totally. The one explosion would encompass both, at once. Under such conditions it makes little difference where the missile is aimed—whether at military or civilian targets. The result is the same in either case: both are simultaneously destroyed.[23]

Nor is discriminate aiming in any sense relevant to the *secondary* effects that would inevitably accompany a nuclear strike. All nuclear weapons—even the smallest—generate poisonous fallout, and the fallout from a megaton burst is deposited over an area of several thousand square miles. It is fatuous to speak of discriminate *aiming* of weapons which, by their inherent nature, have indiscriminate *effects*. It is unlikely that the hundreds of thousands, or perhaps millions, of people who would die lingering deaths from nuclear fallout after such an attack would in any sense appreciate the fine moral scruples of those who had unleashed such wholesale and continuing devastation upon them.[24]

Discriminate aiming in a nuclear war is logically and morally equivalent to using a sledgehammer to kill a fly on someone's head. It is surely possible to kill a fly in this manner; but we must ask: Is it also possible, by any stretch of the imagination, to claim that the ensuing death of the person was only incidental to the death of the fly, or that the smashing of his skull was not included in the intention of the act?[25]

Discriminate aiming is an empty and hence deceptive concept when applied to weapons of such apocalyptic destructiveness as will be used in a thermonuclear war. The difference it denotes does not *make* a difference. Its ultimate effect has been to escalate to ever higher levels the magnitude and fiendishness of violence that men are willing to contemplate as morally acceptable—and, finally, to make it possible for men to commit genocide with a clear conscience.

It must not be supposed, however, that genocide can be achieved only by means of the "big" weapons. There are available any number of "small" (kiloton) nuclear weapons which, if used in sufficient numbers, would serve the purpose equally well. Such weapons—known as "tactical," though they are hundreds of times more destructive than even the "strategic" weapons of thirty years ago (that's progress!)—are designed for "battlefield" use: though it is hard to imagine what, if anything, would be left of such a "battlefield" after a few of those "pineapples" had been dropped on it.

The doctrine of tactical nuclear war was given a great deal of serious attention during the 1950's, particularly in the work of Henry Kissinger, who was perhaps its chief proponent. Since that time it has not been discussed with any regularity or enthusiasm, possibly since none of our allies especially relished the idea of having their territory "defended" by such means,[26] or possibly since we have learned, notably through our Indochinese adventure, that by means of "conventional" weapons we can achieve a level of devastation sufficiently horrendous to render even "small" nuclear weapons unnecessary.[27]

Nevertheless, it should be noted that the doctrine of tactical war, even though moribund, has not by any means been laid to rest. According to Richard Barnet,[28] the United States, as of 1968, had 5,500 nuclear weapons in Southeast Asia—in Korea, Thailand, and on aircraft carriers in the area. Until 1965, he claims, "the Commander in

Chief of the Pacific (CINCPAC) had no plans or weapons capabilities to fight other than a nuclear war in Southeast Asia." [29]

If this is true, it is clear that strategy has been radically overhauled since that time. Yet the question suggests itself: Where are those 5,500 nuclear weapons now? Are there any conditions in Southeast Asia under which they would be used? In view of what has already been done to the land and people of that region with conventional weapons, it is disturbing to consider the immensely greater horrors that would be unleashed against them if nuclear weapons were used.

The rhetoric of nuclear strategy is deceptive. We speak of "limited" war, and are comforted by the traditional associations of that term. Yet the context of destructive power in which such terms are used has been so immensely magnified in the past three decades that what is currently defined as "limited" would have been considered practically *total* thirty years ago. By long exposure we have come to perceive as "commonplace" levels of destructive power that once upon a time were unimaginable. We have learned to "think the unthinkable"—without, however, any significant existential understanding of what the "unthinkable" really means as a human fact. The consequence of this has been to stretch the meaning of such terms as "limited" to the point where they communicate nothing save a deceptive feeling that the world is still in order. Hence, the term "limited" merely serves to screen from awareness the actual destructiveness that even small nuclear weapons would invariably unleash. According to one expert, who is also a spokesman for the use of tactical nuclear weapons:

The development of a quarter-kiloton bomb, which might conceivably be fired from something like a bazooka, would place in the hands of a small team of ground fighters blast charges each on the order of 250 tons of TNT, or equivalent to the explosive power carried by some fifty B-29's in World War II. . . . Cast in forms of adequate flexibility and mobility, fractional kiloton nuclear weapons would represent a potential strength thousands of times greater than ground forces have ever had at their disposal before in the whole history of warfare.[30]

This is quite some escalation of the meaning of "limited" war! It is also a terrifyingly impressive admission. The prospect of every squad leader or every platoon sergeant having in his possession the destructive equivalent of fifty B-29's is not at all reassuring. I cannot conceive that a military engagement fought with weapons of such magnitude could be anything other than an exercise in wholesale carnage. How could anybody defend anything by means of such weapons without inflicting such colossal damage as to nullify the very concept of defense? At the conclusion of such a war, would there be anything left worth coming back to? The picture of tactical war is a picture of nations being "saved" only by being destroyed first.

At any rate, it is not surprising that men conditioned to see any kind of nuclear warfare as "limited" should also have learned without much difficulty to see even the most devastating forms of "conventional" warfare as limited too. Conventional warfare, it appears, is limited simply because it is not nuclear warfare. So habituated have we become to thinking of the ultimate limits of violence in terms of nuclear devastation that we have learned to accept the more circumscribed methods of conventional violence as scarcely problematic at all. Today, in the realm of conventional warfare, practically "anything goes." More than three decades of steadily increasing violence, plus the specter of nuclear incineration, have established the moral context that made possible the grotesque brutalities of the Indochina war. Against the overwhelming reality of the one Big Atrocity—lived with for so long now as to become banal—all the smaller atrocities have lost their power to shock. The simultaneous demise of 100,000 people with a single bomb (Hiroshima) having once been engineered, and the power to dispose of several hundred times that many by much the same means having been subsequently gathered, the haphazard killing of a few thousand Asians per week by means of TNT, napalm, cluster units, or herbicides hardly seems more than trifling by comparison. We unwittingly confess our lost sense of proportion when we lay waste whole villages on the rumor that enemy soldiers *might* have passed through them the day before; when we turn whole provinces into free bombing-and-shooting galleries ("free fire zones") in order to drive the inhabitants into American-run refugee camps where they can be indoctrinated and controlled; when we destroy millions of acres of arable land ostensibly to deny food to enemy soldiers, knowing full well that it is not soldiers but civilians who mostly do the starving; when we defoliate and destroy, in some cases permanently, millions of acres of timber merely to deprive suspected enemy soldiers of a place to hide; when we blanket whole areas with delayed-action cluster bombs which do not go off until the original "suspects" are far away, and other, less cautious, persons are moving about in what they foolishly take to be a safe area.[31] Such atrocities, and the mentality that condones—or at least does not protest—them, are the legacy of thirty years' gradual descent into a technicized barbarism. Guernica, Dresden, Hiroshima, Vietnam: all are milestones on the same tragic road.

## III. The Self-escalating Character of Technology

It is the nature of technology to advance at increasing rates of speed. This is so because it has learned to become very efficient at incorporating into itself its own past achievements, and building upon them. Thus technology is self-escalating, especially when the field to which it is applied offers the promise of unlimited development. As Thomas E. Murray has written:

> As an engineer, I can fully appreciate the seductive attraction exerted by the concept of a technological "open end." Power unlimited is the twentieth-century technician's dream—the counterpart to the fascinating idea of perpetual motion in the nineteenth-century Steam Age. It is the instinct of technology to exploit to the maximum the possibilities inherent in every discovery.[32]

Hence, when technology is turned to the enterprise of weapons development its natural tendency is to produce the most powerful and sophisticated weapons that its present level of expertise makes possible. This tendency is reinforced by what Murray calls "the military planner's perennial quest for the 'irresistible weapon.' " [33] Thus, between the instincts of the engineer and those of the military planner the drive tends to be toward ever more powerful and sophisticated weaponry, as an essentially autonomous, self-justifying process.[34] Therefore, as Murray observes, speaking of the H-bomb development, "weapons technology could not have been expected to control its own instinct." Nevertheless, he asserts, "such control should have been imposed upon it by an over-all strategic policy." [35]

Murray argues at some length the thesis that the shape of U.S. strategic policy in the nuclear age has been essentially determined by the shape of our weaponry, rather than the reverse. The "quest for the irresistible weapon" led to the H-bomb; the H-bomb, in turn, was allowed to impose its own logic upon the direction of policy. "We have been caught in the grip of a technological runaway, and technology itself rather than strategic and moral reason has determined the shape of our weapons program and our defense policy." [36]

> For the last decade or more, our weapons program has been dictated by what we *can* do, scientifically and technologically, rather than by what we *ought* to do, militarily, politically, and morally. Our defense policy has been built backward. Beginning with the existence of multimegaton bombs, it then proceeded to a consideration of factors which rightly should have come first: military strategy and political objectives. The technological tail has been flying the policy kite.[37]

The tendency that Murray describes is immensely exaggerated by the potentially unlimited magnitude of modern (nuclear) weapons. Yet the tendency itself, I believe, is not new. Weapons technology, as noted above, tends to be self-escalating. By its own logic, it seeks ever increasing levels of power and sophistication, regardless of social policy. Despite the limitations of pre-atomic technology, not to mention the irrational conservatism and shortsightedness that have sometimes blinded military planners to new possibilities in the art of killing,[38] it has generally been seen as being in the interest of governments to possess, if not to use, the most advanced weaponry possible.

The more powerful, the better. As former Secretary of Defense Robert McNamara once noted:

> There is a kind of mad momentum intrinsic to the development of all new nuclear weaponry. If a weapons system works—and works well—there is strong pressure from many directions to procure and deploy the weapon out of all proportion to the prudent level required.[39]

Thus it is that the "limits" of war, at any given time, have been determined less by a morality designed to govern and restrain the conduct of war than by a morality in which the *summum bonum* is unimpeded technical advance. What is taken as "legitimate" is conditioned, if not largely determined, by the level of weaponry currently available. What *may* be done is usually decided with reference to what *can* be done. Thus the long process of weapons development, from the hand ax to the H-bomb, represents not simply a technical advance but a steadily escalating assessment as to the morally acceptable limits of war. The ethics of technology, not the ethics of restraint in violence, determine what levels of death and destruction are proportionate to the goals being sought. Technology leads the way, and social ethics follow along behind, making the necessary adjustments.

In "The Limits of Nuclear War," Paul Ramsey wrote:

> So far public opinion in this country seems to ignore the difference between 25,000,000 dead as the probable result of all-out counter-force warfare and 215,000,000 dead as a result of all-out counter-city warfare between the great powers. . . . So, in addition, do we gloss over the qualitative moral distinction between tragically killing or sacrificing human beings as an indirect result of knocking out military targets (counter-force warfare) and the murder-

ous policy of deliberately killing them in totally devastating counter-city warfare.[40]

Ramsey is recognized as one of the most astute analysts of matters having to do with ethics and warfare. He has done as much as any man living to articulate and refine the criteria of discrimination and proportionality for the issue of war in the nuclear age. He is one of the most persistent critics of nuclear policies that would make targets of enemy populations. Yet even his thinking has not escaped the impact of a type of "moral escalation."

The point I wish to emphasize is the way in which weapons themselves have escalated the morally "acceptable" casualty level. A moral calculus fashioned solely with reference to the intrinsic worth of the political objectives involved might conceivably have concluded that 25 million corpses, even "indirectly" exterminated, are a disportionate sacrifice—thus making nuclear war itself an *un*acceptable choice. But Ramsey does not do this; what is morally "acceptable" to him seems to be whatever level of devastation the weapons themselves, by their present magnitude, happen to impose, just so long as they are used in a "counter-force" capacity.

Thus it seems to me that Ramsey is a moralist whose concept of the "acceptable" has escalated under the impact of technology. His position seems to have changed rather markedly since 1961, when he published *War and the Christian Conscience*. In the earlier book, he wrote:

> I confess I find it difficult to imagine a limited use of hydrogen weapons, especially if smaller, even fractional kiloton weapons would be just as destructive of legitimate military targets and less indirectly destructive of civil life. I think, therefore, that we have to say that megaton weapons would always destroy military objectives only incidental to

the destruction of a whole area; and that in the very weapon itself, its use, its possession, or the threat to use it, warfare has passed beyond all reasonable or justifiable limits.[41]

Since that time, Ramsey has radically escalated his assessment of the "justifiable limits" of war to include the use of megaton weapons, as long as these weapons are used in a "counter-force" (hence, discriminating) capacity.

In 1962, Ramsey discussed the principle of "double effect" [42] in the following terms:

It was never supposed that non-combatants were morally immune from indirect injury or death *on however colossal a scale,* if there is proportionate grave reason for doing this.[43]

The willingness to accept "collateral" destruction "on however colossal a scale" has become, it seems, a moral sanction for large-scale nuclear war. Ramsey is able thereby to accept wholesale nuclear destruction as morally viable so long as this destruction is inflicted for "proportionate grave reason" as well as not by "direct intent."

What makes this argument problematic is the difficulty in determining just what constitutes a "proportionate grave reason." A "proportionate grave reason" is presumably one that is justified either (1) by the avoidance of a consequence even worse than that of wholesale nuclear devastation, or (2) by the achievement of a political objective so transcendently desirable that the good to be had through its possession would overbalance the evil of the destruction imposed in obtaining it. Unfortunately such comparisons contain an element of subjectivity that makes highly suspect any moral calculation based on them. The only consequence that is clearly *objectively* worse than wholesale

nuclear devastation is *greater* wholesale nuclear devastation.[44] All other comparisons, involving the achievement
or the dispossession of other (e.g., political) objectives, involve the imposition of value judgments. This is hardly
avoidable, of course; ultimately, *all* human judgments are
value judgments. Yet, what is problematic in this case is the
tendency for value judgments to be distorted by the increasing acceptability of mass violence.

As one is conditioned, by existing circumstances, to
accept increasing levels of violence as legitimate, he must
by that very fact be led to accept objectives of decreasing
gravity as justifying such violence.[45] One's judgment as to
what constitutes "proportionate grave reason" for the waging of war, including thermonuclear war, must be determined in large measure by the *level* of violence that he is
willing to accept as a valid price for *any* objective. The
intent of this chapter has been to show that the levels of
violence that men are presently willing to accept have
escalated sharply since the late 1930's under the impact
(1) of the violence that has actually occurred during that
time, and (2) of the weapons that have made it possible.

Paul Ramsey's hypothetical choice between 25 million
dead (killed "morally") and 215 million dead (killed "im-
morally") is a choice between wholesale nuclear devastation and greater wholesale nuclear devastation. If we have,
indeed, reached such a pass that a grotesque choice like
this threatens to become our only option, then it might not
be altogether presumptuous to conclude that the system of
assumptions and policies that has led us into it is morally
bankrupt. Such a system needs to be abandoned in favor
of one that does not threaten to destroy either the physical
existence or the fundamental humanity of the race.

## 5.

## HORROR DOMESTICATED:
## THE SEMANTICS OF MEGADEATH

IT SHOULD BE EVIDENT BY NOW THAT WE ARE DEALING NOT merely with the shape of *policy* but with the quality of *consciousness*. Moral decision-making is not strictly an "intellectual" process; it reflects a total response of the self. Any moral transformation is also a transformation of consciousness. Thus, to "escalate the acceptable" is to alter prevailing sensitivities regarding the nature and value of human life and the intentional killing of other men.

Therefore mass-destruction weapons must be judged, by their very nature, as corrupting the quality of human consciousness. This corruption, which is partly ethical, is also partly semantic. The nature of mass-destruction weapons generates a kind of semantic disorder, reflected in radically distorted relationships between language and reality. This distortion is not simply verbal. The structure of language reflects the structure of thought. Hence any serious pathology in the realm of *meanings* is more than a problem of language; it is a problem of *consciousness*.

It is a mistake to suppose that problems connected with language and meaning are peripheral to the major concerns of human living. On the contrary, they are central. A number of students have preferred to define man as the symbol-using animal.[1] It is their reasoned conviction that the development and use of systems of symbolized meaning are the one factor that most fully characterizes and determines the level of human existence. As Henry N. Wieman puts it:

> Man is distinguished from everything else by this outstanding characteristic: he accumulates symbolized meaning so that the past rolls up into the present like a snowball. Not only is this true of the individual as he develops from infancy; it is true of the human race as it has developed from its beginnings until now. Furthermore, the individual human being reaches a high level of development to the degree that he is able to accumulate symbolized meanings throughout his own history.[2]

All animals use "language" and express "meaning," but the differences in this respect between the animal level and the human level are decisive.

1. Animal language consists of *signs;* a sign carries a meaning that is attached to a local, concrete situation, and cannot be detached from it. The animal reacts, always, to its immediate situation; what it "says" is attached, inextricably, to the objects or events that it confronts directly. It cannot tell us about something that happened yesterday, or in some other locale; it can tell us only about what is happening here and now. "Man" is always *this* man; the event is always *this* event.

Human language, by contrast, consists of *symbols;* the meanings carried by symbols are detachable: they can stand alone. They can be lifted out of the local situation in such a way as to designate whole classes of things and events not immediately present. All human thinking and speaking is a process of symbol manipulation detached from specific content up to, and including, the creation of structures of meaning having no actual existence in the world of space and time. Through this process, man is able to liberate himself from the tyranny of a life bounded by the limitations of immediate, firsthand realities.

2. Animal language is a language solely of emotional expression. An animal can tell us nothing about the object, or the event, that it confronts; it can only express its own subjective reaction. It can tell us, in effect: "I'm happy"; "I'm sad"; "I'm angry"; "I'm afraid"; "I'm excited"; etc. But it can tell us nothing about the object or the event that makes it feel that way. Moreover, because its language is not detachable from the immediate situation, it can say to us, "I *am* happy" or "I *am* sad," but never "I *was* happy" or "I *was* sad."

Human language, on the other hand, is both subjective and objective: it is able to convey information about the world beyond the self which does the speaking. The liberation is therefore twofold: from the tyranny of the immediate and from the prison of pure subjectivity.

Thus, the two most important facts about human language are: (1) it is detachable from the immediate situation, and (2) it is able to encompass the external world. These two factors are decisive in making possible the distinctively human level of existence. This is true in the following ways:

*a.* Symbolization expands the range of "information" available to man beyond the scope of his own firsthand experience. The most significant information that man has does not come directly to him from the "world"; it comes to him through other minds in the form of symbolized meaning. (This community of minds, with their networks of symbolized meaning, is for man the most important part of the world.) This information may designate facts about the world; it may designate interpretations or theories; it may designate events or relations having no space-time existence (fiction, mathematics, logic, myth, scientific constructs, etc.). In this way, symbolization may be thought of as a doorway into larger perceptions of reality.

*b.* Symbolization is a medium of contact with other minds. Thus it makes possible the kind of relationship or association distinctively human, in which persons and groups are able to create a "common world" by sharing with each other wide ranges of experience and meaning otherwise accessible only to themselves separately. This growing context of shared meaning is wider and richer than the world of separate existence; as it grows, it creates wider and deeper community.

*c.* Symbolization makes possible the storing of shared information; thus knowledge is able to increase over the passage of time, making it possible for each new generation to commence where the previous generation left off. This cumulative deposit of organized meaning, otherwise called "culture," forms the substance of art, religion, philosophy, science, technology, social organization, and institutions generally—everything, in fact, that makes human life uniquely human.

*d.* Thus the world as humanly experienced is qualitatively unique. It is a world organized symbolically, in which the crucial dimensions are not "objects" or "events" but *meanings*. These meanings are in no sense peripheral to human life; they form the very substance of consciousness itself. If they were taken away, man would no longer be human; he would be little more than a biological organism. In fact, even his biological organism could not survive:

[H]is organism has become so adapted to the exercise of symbolized meaning in getting the necessities of life that the body could not care for itself if it were deprived of the human mind with its symbols.[3]

Thus it is no exaggeration to suggest that symbolization and communication are the fundamental, distinctively human, acts.

Since symbolization and communication are two of the ultimate factors that make human life human, it makes sense to speak of them as fundamentally "good." This does not mean, however, that *every instance* of symbolization or communication is "good." What is "essentially" good can, under certain conditions, become evil. This is true of symbolization, which, like most human realities, can be used either creatively or destructively. Through symbolization, we can build up or tear down, enhance or subvert, enlighten or mislead, heal or injure.

Man does not have access to unmediated perception of reality "as it is," whatever that may mean. The world as humanly perceived is a world organized by systems of symbolized meaning; these are the "filters" through which man perceives the world, and there is no way in which he can escape them. He can exchange one set of filters for another, but he cannot escape using *some* filters. This means that reality as humanly perceived is the product of a process in which man himself participates; it does not mean that reality is purely a "subjective" construction of the human mind. True and false, right and wrong, are not subject merely to human decision; they are coercive. They have an objective component against which our truth claims and value claims have to be measured.

The essential function of language is to reveal reality.

Language functioning properly does this, in the several ways described above. But language often functions in just the opposite fashion, by serving as an instrument of falsehood and self-deception. It may do this in a number of ways: for example, through misstatement of fact; through interpretations or theories that distort the relationships and the implications of facts; through reifying the symbolic constructions of imagination, as if they had an objective existence of their own; through language whose primary associations are radically incongruent with the realities designated.

The ability, through symbolization, to transcend and thus to liberate the imagination from the grasp of immediate, firsthand realities is crucial for human life, but it functions properly only if we are able, at any given moment, to focus back down through our symbol constructions at the world itself. Any process of high-order abstraction that remains too severely or too long detached from its existential content runs the risk of becoming dangerously pathological. A focus that too consistently transcends the world of heavy, nonverbal reality tends to erode sensitivity to much of what is actually, concretely "there." When this happens, language becomes a vehicle of emotional detachment, or a means of concealing certain crucial aspects of first-order reality.

One crucial consequence of the nuclear age has been to introduce into the human arena weapons whose potential effects are, in a sense, not merely human but cosmic. Such effects transcend the limits both of imagination and of language; in their full reality they are literally "unfeelable" and inexpressible. The human organism is incapable of summoning a depth of feeling even remotely proportionate to the reality of mass extermination, and there are simply no words in existence that are able to convey *both* the objective fact *and* the full reality of its human impact. The simultaneous extermination of 100 million people, or even one million, is a concept essentially devoid of human meaning. We can imagine—we can respond to—the death of one person, or even of several persons; by no possible extrapolation can we even begin to grasp the death of millions as a single event. We can denote the fact itself, simply as a raw datum; we can say, as a matter of statistical prediction, that 25 million or 50 million or 100 million people will be killed on the first day of a nuclear war. But these words are essentially empty of content; there is almost no humanly appreciable connection between the abstraction they embody and the indescribably colossal human realities to which they ultimately refer.

Thus, in the nuclear age we are compelled to deal with realities for which there can be no satisfactory language. All discussion requires the use of words, yet the only words available to discuss nuclear realities are either (1) drawn from human situations of much narrower scope, or (2) so abstract as to be existentially empty. In the first instance the traditional meanings of the words are often radically incongruent with the new realities to which they refer; in the second instance these realities are translated into a network of high-level abstractions devoid of human meaning. In both cases the language used is semantically corrupting: it conceals humanly crucial dimensions of reality.

In his famous essay "Politics and the English Language," George Orwell observed how language, without resorting to deliberate misstatement of fact, can nevertheless be used to hide or distort the truth. "In our times," he said, "political speech and writing are largely the defense of the indefensible":

Thus political language has to consist largely of euphemisms, question-begging and sheer cloudy vagueness. Defenseless villages are bombarded from the air, the inhabitants driven out into the countryside, the cattle machine-gunned, the huts set on fire with incendiary bullets: this is called *pacification*. Millions of peasants are robbed of their farms and sent trudging along the roads with no more than they can carry: this is called *transfer of population* or *rectification of frontiers*. People are imprisoned for years without trial, or shot in the back of the neck or sent to die of scurvy in Arctic lumber camps: this is called *elimination of undesirable elements*. Such phraseology is needed if one wants to name things without calling up mental pictures of them.[4]

In the rhetoric of nuclear strategy, a similar debasement of language has taken place. The rhetoric cited by Orwell is deliberately concocted for the express purpose of deception. This is probably true also of the rhetoric of nuclear strategy. The very nature of nuclear weapons is such as to encourage such debasement—indeed, to make it virtually inevitable. Given the initial thrust, the makers of rhetoric in the nuclear age have shown no small measure of ingenuity in devising a jargon whose purpose and effect is to render the concept of nuclear war emotionally palatable. In the service of this objective, the existential realities of nuclear holocaust are concealed or distorted by surrounding them with a pink cloud of familiar and reassuring verbal tags. Because of their deceptive character in seeming to convey information but actually concealing it instead, I call such euphemisms "anti-information." (The term, I believe, was originated by S. I. Hayakawa.) A number of examples follow:

1. *Clean bomb*. A projectile which, while destroying mil-

lions of people, will deposit little fallout. One thinks of scrubbed skin or of freshly done laundry, and the realities of mass death are successfully camouflaged.

2. *Bonus.* If an attack is launched on a missile site and a nearby city is wiped out in addition, the latter is a "bonus" —something nice thrown in, as it were, free of charge.

3. *Nukes.* Could anything be more deceptive than to christen weapons of mass destruction with such diminutive and affectionate labels as this?

4. *Sunshine unit.* Strontium 90. Note the association of robust good health. Underlying message: Radioactivity is good for you.

5. *Hound-dog; Bambi.* Names of missiles. Underlying message: Don't be afraid of nuclear missiles; they're really cute, harmless little things.

6. *To lob* (*a missile*). "Could anything be more deceptive than to speak of a missile that travels thousands of miles in less than a quarter of an hour as being 'lobbed'?" [5]

7. *Minuteman.* "It relieves the conscience to be able to think of 950 Minutemen guarding our frontiers; the burden of guilt might be insupportable if we weighed in our minds that each Minuteman is a 54-foot missile weighing over 32 tons and armed with a destructive device 30 times more powerful than the bomb that destroyed Hiroshima." [6]

8. *Nuclear umbrella.* What could be more suggestive of the safe, ordinary world of daily living than an umbrella?

9. *Nuclear hardware.* What could be more cozily domestic than this reference to the kitchen?

10. *Margin of superiority.* Distinctions of superiority-inferiority carry associations of the ordinary human world in which such distinctions have a measurable human meaning (e.g., as in the comparison of two football teams— even two armies). When used to compare relative magni-

tudes of nuclear destructiveness, they refer to nothing humanly appreciable.

11. *Limited war.* As already noted in Chapter 4, this phrase conveys a false reassurance because it skims over the fact that even "limited" nuclear war is still a war of indescribably horrendous devastation.

It is not surprising that the Indochina holocaust, which was as close to being total as anything short of nuclear war could be, developed its own arsenal of sadistically innocuous abstractions. To wit:

12. *Anti-personnel weapons.* Cannisters of metal or plastic shrapnel designed exclusively for use against people. They are intended, not so much to kill, as to maim— since wounded people tie up more resources than dead ones. Plastic shrapnel, unlike metal, has the added advantage of being undetectable by X-rays. Such weapons are actually anti-*people;* "personnel" is a handy abstraction designed to conceal the human reality of those on the receiving end. It is also designed to convey the absolutely false impression that these weapons are used only against soldiers (soldiers are "personnel"; civilians are simply "people").

13. *Pineapple; Guava; Butterfly.* Anti-personnel weapons. In the "ordinary" world of non-war, pineapples, guavas, and butterflies do not blow off limbs or riddle the body with shrapnel.

14. *Bouncing Betty.* Another anti-personnel weapon—a small mine that bounces up to explode in the victim's face. Bouncing Betty might more likely be a favorite childhood toy or pet—surely not something designed to blow a man's head off.

15. *Fat Albert.* A powerful air-to-ground missile. The chummy familiarity of its name (one almost wants to say

"his" name) scarcely conveys the reality of what it is and what it can do to anything it hits.

16. *Hosing.* An affectionate euphemism for aerial machine-gunning. Note the cozily domestic association with cleaning the car or watering the lawn. The reality, of course, is quite different: machine guns such as were used on American aircraft in Indochina fire more than 100 rounds *per second;* a mere instant of such "hosing" quite literally reduces a human being to "a pile of bloody rags." [7]

17. *Barbecueing.* Another association drawn from the "good life" of backyard American suburbia. This one refers of course to the fire-bombing of villages by American planes.

18. *Kill ratio; Body count.* Terms like these seek to reduce the hideous realities of organized killing to an exercise in technical problem-solving, without serious human connection.

19. *Sanitize.* An area was said to be "sanitized" when all supporters of the Vietcong had been killed, captured, or relocated. This term and the implicit metaphor of a germ-free environment betray the dehumanized attitude of Americans toward those whom they define as "enemy." Of equal interest is the way in which the American passion for personal cleanliness has become linked with the conduct of warfare: Americans have learned to accept a state of more or less continuous killing as acceptable, as long as the killing does not involve the killers themselves in any direct, personal, physical way. It is the triumph of modern technology to have made such killing the normative pattern.

Words and phrases of the type examined above are nuclear age examples of semantic corruption—which means, in the final analysis, corruption of consciousness.

They are designed to conceal the awful realities of modern war by investing them with positive associations drawn from the safer, more pleasant world of daily existence. The consequence of this practice can only be increasingly to domesticate the horrors of modern war, up to and including nuclear incineration, and thus to render these horrors more palatable. In this way, semantic corruption conspires with other factors to "escalate the acceptable."

Since the late 1950's a group of scholars, of whom Herman Kahn is perhaps the most famous, have given full time to the task of analyzing and writing about nuclear strategy. The works of these men contain a number of common features that are germane to this discussion. To begin with, they accept as more or less axiomatic the assumption that nuclear weapons are efficacious in deterring general war; yet the bulk of their work concerns the possible "scenarios" that might obtain if deterrence were to fail. This realistic awareness that deterrence is not infallible impels them, as their major intellectual task, to select and picture the worst, to "think about the unthinkable"—to spell out in some detail the possible futures that might obtain under conditions of actual nuclear warfare. Yet these possible futures are seldom if ever defined in terms of what actually happens to people. They are defined, for the most part, in terms of "strategy" considerations alone, of moves and countermoves, based largely on game-theory models. Thus the literature of nuclear strategy largely explores situations whose human significance is unimaginably frightful, yet in doing so it uses words that are essentially empty of human meaning.

It is not surprising that men who spend their lives writing about nuclear war should develop a rather casual and detached attitude toward the more grisly elements of their subject—especially since none of the scenarios they write about are, at the moment, anything more than elaborate speculative fictions. Events of such apocalyptic magnitude carry a meaning that is quite beyond the capacity of any human imagination to grasp. There is simply no way to relate to them as truly human events. Thus, the more horrendous the subject, the more compelling the temptation to deal with it purely as an abstraction without human content.

To illustrate this, I have selected an extended passage more or less at random from an article by Herman Kahn:

Let us consider now an extreme and continuing provocation—say, an all-out invasion of A by B limiting himself to the use of conventional or even tactical nuclear weapons. Assume also that A cannot resist B's invasion with his own tactical forces. If the nuclear show of force indicated . . . above did not stop the invasion, it has been suggested that one tactic a desperate or enraged A might employ would be to destroy one of B's cities and threaten to continue destroying a city a day until B backs down. At this point B would have several choices. He could, of course, back down and sign a peace treaty ending the limited general war. He could threaten to destroy two cities for one, initiating an exchange that would be likely to escalate further. Or he could threaten to destroy only one city for one and say: "I will continue until you stop this insane city destruction," meanwhile continuing his invasion. The one-city-for-one is not only costly; it carries with it a risk of further escalation, but clearly less risk than the two-for-one reprisal. The backdown is of course least likely to escalate. If B does decide to back down, he might just sue for peace or ask for a cease-fire, or he might not do so until he had destroyed a city of A's and announced: "In the face of your insane behavior, I have decided to compromise, but you did not get a free ride by forcing me to do so. You, too, lost a city, so do not use this as a precedent in the future. If you try it again, the same thing will happen, and even though you win the issue, you will lose a city in doing so. Possibly the next time you will prefer not to attack, but to withdraw, or negotiate a peace."

In some circumstances, A might go ahead and destroy another city in revenge, but in most circumstances it is hard to believe that he would retaliate in turn. Although A might wish to do so to establish a precedent, the precedent is hardly worth the added risk. No matter how justified A might feel, B is unlikely to let A get away with it. B is too likely both to be enraged and to feel that acquiescence would be the end of B's bargaining power, because A will feel that B will have to give way in the future even if B does not actually believe he has to. And, indeed, B's fears may be justified. Letting A get away with extra damage is likely to encourage A to believe in A's potency and B's weakness.[8]

This passage exhibits the character of much nuclear age rhetoric. It outlines a sequence of possible events which, if actually occurring, would be humanly catastrophic. Yet the passage itself reflects none of this. In its breezy, casual style, its detached emotional tone, and its rhetoric of gamesmanship, it tends to suggest that nuclear war is scarcely more savage than an unusually arduous chess match between unfriendly opponents. Nowhere do the language, the style, or the emotional tone reflect the fact that "city-swapping" is a sequence in which untold millions of people would be consigned to a horrible—and essentially meaningless—death. The subject here is not chess: it is mass murder.

The work of Kahn, and of men like him, doubtless has some value; but, whatever its value, it has not escaped a form of semantic corruption: it is existentially empty. Thus it conceals humanly crucial dimensions of reality. In the words of Justus George Lawler: "The incineration of all life is never really faced; what *is* faced are the academic problems of the algebra of killing, the problems of adjusting, equating, and manipulating the well-bred symbols of annihilation." [9]

Semantic corruption represents a distortion of consciousness—a dissociation between the symbolized abstractions of human discourse and the realities to which they refer. This dissociation, as we have seen, is widely observable in the rhetoric of the nuclear age. Given the nature of modern war and the weapons that shape it, the result could scarcely be otherwise.

# 6.

# ANTISEPTIC WAR: THE PROBLEM OF PERSONAL RESPONSIBILITY

A SENSE OF RESPONSIBILITY FOR OTHER PERSONS AND FOR THE nature and destiny of the common life is crucial to the existence of any human society. Without it, there would be no "society," properly speaking—only an aggregation of independent individuals.

The most basic meaning of responsibility is *the ability to respond.* It is the capacity to be affected by what happens to others. One does not merely observe the fate of others, from a distance as it were; he sees his own life as bound up with theirs. He sees himself as being "involved." Thus the second meaning of responsibility is the recognition of personal *involvement.* It is the awareness that one is not "separate"; his life belongs inextricably to the brotherhood of all human lives. "No man is an island, entire of itself; every man is a piece of the continent, a part of the main." He exists only in relation to others; these relationships are not external to him: they form the very substance of his being. Thus, finally, responsibility is the recognition that one is *accountable.* Our actions do not "belong" to us alone, for their impact does not stop at the boundary of our own lives. What we do, or fail to do, makes a difference, for good or ill, in the lives of others. Hence, in the final analysis, to be responsible is to acknowledge that we are called upon, by the very nature of things (which some men call "God"), to govern our lives with reference, not merely to ourselves alone, but to the sum total of the lives of all upon whom the consequences of our actions fall.

The purpose of this chapter is to examine the impact of mass-destruction weapons upon the awareness and the exercise of responsibility, both personal and corporate.

A man feels morally responsible, for the most part, if there is some visible connection between his decisions and their consequences. I had known, for example, for some time, that much of the money which the Government exacted from me in taxes eventually ended up as bullets or shrapnel in the bodies of Indochinese peasants. Yet, try as I would, I could not cause myself to feel the same degree of responsibility for this fact as I would have felt if it were I myself who had actually been doing the killing. My connection with the final result, *though every bit as real*, was indirect and invisible. Other people were actually doing the killing; they were committing the actions that took life. I did nothing; therefore the sense of responsibility that I ought realistically to have felt was much attenuated. I *should* have felt responsible but I did not, except in a kind of abstract, theoretical way. This is probably why draft resistance tends to command more urgency than tax refusal as a form of antiwar protest. The soldier must actually *do* "the dirty work"; the civilian merely *pays* for it —as if those who do the paying were not every bit as involved and every bit as guilty as those who do the shooting.

This illustrates a moral problem that is characteristic of mass-destruction weapons. To begin with, mass-destruction weapons systems are so fantastically complex that their development and manufacture require the ministrations of vast armies of highly specialized experts. Each participant, we may suppose, knows in the long run that he is making engines of mass destruction; yet whatever sense of personal responsibility he might feel must be seriously blunted by the immense separation between his own narrow specialty and the finished product. His own immediate pursuit is the only part of the whole with which he is permitted to have any firsthand acquaintance. The finished product he may never see—certainly he will never see it in action; its existence and purpose are remote, abstract, unreal. One sees himself as a specialist in gyromechanisms, microcircuitry, or plasma physics; he does not think of himself as an engineer of mass destruction.

> The guilt of killing is spread so thin—shared so universally —that it no longer seems personal. Would the General who pressed the button launching an ICBM be more guilty than the Sergeant who helped prepare it for firing? Or the physicist who designed the guidance system? Or the mathematician who programmed the computer? Or the worker who poured concrete for the missile's underground silo? Or the Chicago housewife working in a factory who soldered together the electrical components for the guidance system?
>
> Was ever the taking of life so clinical, so aseptic, so far removed from personal blame?[1]

In situations involving the manufacture and use of mass-destruction weapons, major decisions are made not by one person alone but by numerous individuals and machines acting more or less in series. The total decision is not reducible to that of any single person; it stands as the sum of several decisions, none of which can be designated as the crucial one. Under such conditions the sense of responsibility cannot but suffer a severe attenuation. When all are responsible, no one is responsible. Thus, in a sense, personal responsibility is transferred to the organization or the machine:

> Let us assume that the bomb has been exploded.
>
> To call this "an action" is inappropriate. The chain of events leading up to the explosion is composed of so many links, the process has involved so many different agencies, so many intermediate steps and partial actions, none of which is the crucial one, that in the end no one can be regarded as the agent. Everyone has a good conscience, because no conscience was required at any point. . . .
>
> Even where robots are not resorted to, the monstrous undertaking is immensely facilitated by the fact that it is not carried out by individuals, but by a complex and vastly ramified organization. . . . Each participant, each intermediary, performs or has insight into only the job assigned to him; and certainly each works conscientiously. The specialized worker is not conscious of the fact that the conscientious efforts of a number of specialists can add up to the most monstrous lack of conscience: just as in any other industrial enterprise he has no insight into the process as a whole.[2]

This is why it is possible for essentially "decent" men— men of good conscience, goodwill, good intentions—working together, nonetheless to produce, as the sum of their collective efforts, the most inhuman forms of evil. The whole is *not* merely the sum of its parts.

The development of weaponry—from the hand ax to the hydrogen bomb—has been characterized by steadily increasing destructiveness, impersonality, and distance between combatants. A hand weapon—the club, the spear, the sword, even the bow and arrow—required close contact with the enemy and was able to kill only one person at a time. The introduction of the musket extended the killing range to a distance limited only by visibility, while the development of artillery increased the range to several miles and radically expanded the number of people that could be destroyed with a single shot. With the introduction of artillery, then of aircraft, it became possible, with a minimum of physical exertion or personal involvement, to kill more people at much greater distances: including people that one could not even see, people whose very existence, in fact, was unknown to those doing the killing. Finally, the development of nuclear missile systems has increased the distance from miles to continents, and expanded the magnitude of potential destruction to apocalyptic proportions. At long last, it is possible by the mere flick of a switch to annihilate millions of people on the other side of the earth with almost literally no physical or emotional input and in virtually total isolation from one's victims and the results of one's act.

Thus, in the nuclear age, technology has made possible a radically new kind of killing. It is now possible to kill more easily, more efficiently, more totally, and with less personal involvement, than ever before in the history of man. Killing in the nuclear age is no longer a "personal" act; it is no longer something that someone "does." One does not really kill; he merely presses a switch, and killing, as it were, takes place—somewhere far off and out of sight.

Thus, the nuclear age warrior is a very different kind of man from his predecessors. In the words of Anatol Rapoport:

The warrior has become a component in a "weapons system." He sits at the controls *in comfort,* as a clerk sits at his desk. He watches signals which convey commands

totally devoid of drama. He hears no battle cries, no ex-
hortations to bravery and sacrifice. He is not asked to face
a withering fire or to charge the enemy. He obeys only the
little colored lights that go on and off on his panels. Death
may reach him at any moment, of course, but in this
respect the situation of the hero is exactly the same as that
of the coward. Neither of them looks death in the face;
neither can run away. There are no heroes, only victims.
The "ideal" of nuclear war is the complete automation of
slaughter.[3]

It is essential that we examine very carefully the moral
implications of this bizarre and thoroughly unparalleled
situation. To get the full impact of the problem, we might
at this point recount a story told by Fr. Philip Berrigan,
S.S.J. The story, incidentally, is purported to be true.

[T]he story is told of two young men who might be described as silo-sitters. They are clad in spotless white
over-alls, each wears a .45 automatic on his hip, each
wears a badge with the motto, "Aggressor Beware," each
has a key, which at the command of authority reaching
back to [the President], can together turn a lock to hurl
out of the ground more explosives than have been fired
in all the wars of the world's history. Smith and Jones, we
might call them, command 10 Minuteman missiles buried
in 80 ft. concrete silos in South Dakota; capable of 500
times the explosive force which hit Hiroshima 20 years ago.
The Minutemen are programmed by electronic computer
for Russian cities. Jones, an Air Force Capt., was asked
how it would feel to receive the order to fire and to turn
the key. He smiled and said that "it's no different than
going home and turning the key in the front door." [4]

The intent of this story is not to castigate the "silo-
sitters" as moral monsters ( except in the sense that we have
*all* become moral monsters); there is no reason to suppose

them any more bloodthirsty or less humane than the mass of men generally. Yet it is just this fact which renders the situation so frightful. The technology at their fingertips makes it possible for these men to wreak indiscriminate and absolutely apocalyptic violence upon untold numbers of unseen victims with no physical effort and no personal involvement whatever. Thus we are faced with a terrible irony: that through the power of a mindless technology, otherwise "good" men are made, potentially, the casual doers of evil thousands of times more devilish, more hideous, than the most vicious or demented person could ever perform by his own powers alone.

These men clearly have been placed in a situation whose impact is itself morally destructive. A man feels responsible, as noted earlier, if there is some visible connection between his acts and their consequences. But it is just this connection which is broken by the present structure of weapons technology. When it is possible by the mere turning of a key or the pressing of a switch to annihilate whole cities, the fantastic disproportion between the human effort required and the results that ensue cannot fail to destroy in large measure the felt connection between decisions and their consequences. Turning the key or pressing the switch are such minute, simple acts. Psychologically it is difficult to identify them as acts of aggression, yet their consequences transcend by thousands of times the highest intensity of psychological aggression that one can possibly envision. As Anatol Rapoport observes:

> The more destructive the weapons and the more efficient the apparatus of triggering them, the smaller is the degree of willingness required to put them to use. . . . The magnitude of the destruction would be quite unrelated to the intensity of hatred of the opponents for each other.[5]

Indeed, under these conditions, there need be no hatred; pressing the deadly button is too simple an act to require any feelings at all. This, in fact, is the danger.

The psychic disconnection between acts and their results is complicated, in advanced weapons technology, by a dissociation or distance between people. One is isolated in every possible sense from the "enemy." He does not see or hear them. He does not know or care who they are. He does not even know whether they exist. They may be several hundred or even several thousand miles away. They are anonymous, faceless; they have no personal identity; they possess no existential reality for him. They are present to him, if at all, only through the strength of moral imagination. And sad to say, moral imagination is a factor of which there does not seem to be an overly abundant supply in this world.[6]

Under conditions of modern technology, killing is impersonal and anonymous—and therefore, to that extent, *easier to do*. Those with the task of killing have been separated, in every possible way, from their victims and from the results of their own acts.[7] Under such conditions, we may suppose, it would be almost impossible to believe that one had actually done anything so hideous as to annihilate several million human beings. There would, after all, be *no really meaningful evidence*—only readings on a dial. A person would be spared the sight of corpses in the streets, the screams of the dying would not reach his ears, nor would the stink of burning flesh touch his nostrils. None of these things would move him, because they would not reach him. They would not bring to him the reality of what he had actually done.

It is ironic that an age so skilled in the technology of practically instantaneous communication should be the context for such massive dissociation from existential human realities on the part of men who by their activity may, or actually do, exercise such massive impact on those realities. This fact is due to the nature of the medium. Communications, in the context of weapons technology or military engagement, are for the most part the translation of first-order events into electronic abstractions. By this process, human realities on the receiving end of a weapon are experienced at the firing end simply as "data": electronic signals, radar blips, computer readouts, etc. Such "communications" communicate nothing existentially real. For the men who monitor such systems, "the radar blip and flashing lights no more represent human beings than the tokens in a board-type war game. War and war games become much the same." [8]

It is clear that men whose primary task is to monitor and interpret electronic data cannot be considered, in any existential sense, "soldiers." They are technicians.[9] Objectively, they are one link in a chain of cause and effect whose end product, actually or potentially, is massive death and destruction. Experientially, they are manipulators of machines and interpreters of electronic symbolisms. For men in this position, the activities in which they engage must become, very largely, ends in themselves, thus giving to the enterprise of death a sense of unreality.

The use of complex gadgetry and the acquisition of the skills to operate it successfully can endow the entire destructive process with the characteristics of a game. The mere manipulation of the machinery is absorbing and pleasurable, like playing with a super-sophisticated pinball machine. The effects or merits of the actions are not considered; if such questions arise at all, they are dismissed as matters for high-level decision of no legitimate concern to those who execute the commands.[10]

It should be especially emphasized that we are not now referring exclusively to *nuclear* weapons systems. While nuclear systems, by their very nature, led the way, the automation of weapons has been moving increasingly onto the "battlefield," where "conventional" war is being fought. Since the late 1960's, the Indochina war witnessed the rapid growth of new automated weaponry, referred to collectively as the "electronic battlefield." As its name suggests, the electronic battlefield represents an attempt to give the tactical direction of aerial warfare as far as possible to complex machine-systems that automatically select the targets and fly the planes. Some descriptions of the technology currently in force read like science fiction:

Half a world away from America one of the strangest wars in history, and the first of its type, is being waged. Generals in command of forces engaging the enemy study computer readouts instead of battle maps to determine their tactics. Pilots who fly the mission set coordinates into aircraft computers; planes fly automatically and release their bombs by electronic signal. . . .

High above the battlefield unmanned aircraft circle, their insides packed with electronic equipment which picks up and silently retransmits signals from transmitters that were earlier embedded into the ground (at 600 mph!) and still continue to function—yet self-destruct if man tries to move one. The signals transmitted from the ground transmitters to the drones overhead go to some of the world's largest computers. Then machines, not man, perform the calculations of thousands of variables. A mad metal ball hammers out the probable reactions or options available to other men who, hundreds of miles away, ponder the next move. . . .

Only in this war can you find the veterans of a hundred computer battles who have never heard a shot fired, pilots who bomb acres, not pinpoints, and fly by computer, bombs which drop on electronic signal, drones that fly without manual control—and the entire system tied to a collection of tubes, transistors and diodes that calculate time and space with the precision of an astronaut's moon landing. Except that the objective may be the next rest stop for a convoy traveling through Laos.[11]

What is the objective of such a system? Three possible answers are suggested. (1) To increase the efficiency of target selection by replacing human senses wherever possible with machines that can "see" where human senses cannot (either by acting as extensions of human sensory capacity or by going where human beings cannot go: i.e., into enemy territory). (2) To increase the speed and "objectivity" of target-data interpretation (by eliminating human "subjectivity").[12] (3) To increase the speed and accuracy of weapons delivery onto the target (improved "real time" response).

The effect of all this is, wherever possible, "to replace men with machines." Specifically, this means (1) to decrease as far as possible the amount of "human input" required for system functioning, especially in the interpretation of data, and (2) to remove all human agents in the system as far as possible from the "battle" area, either horizontally, to bases on the periphery, or vertically, in the cockpits of high-flying bombers.

Clearly, warfare carried on in such a manner as this is a recipe for practically unlimited and indiscriminate violence: unlimited because unrestrained by any sense of human reality at the other end of the weapons; indiscriminate because dependent upon the judgment, either of machines which cannot discriminate between friend and enemy,[13] or of men who have, by their insulation from human reality, been robbed of any sense of urgency in the *making* of discriminate judgments.[14]

The ultimate objective implicit in warfare of this kind is the total automation of killing. It carries the vision of warfare conducted exclusively "by proxy"[15]: all the troops have "come home," and the land has been blanketed by sensing devices, while unmanned computerized aircraft, directed by technicians hundreds of miles from the battle zone, continue to rain fire and death on the enemy below.[16]

That some such vision is indeed part of current military thinking is clear from statements already being made on the subject. According to General William Westmoreland:

> On the battlefield of the future, enemy forces will be located, tracked, and targeted almost instantaneously through the use of data links, computer assisted intelligence evaluation, and automated fire control. With first round kill probabilities approaching certainty, and with surveillance devices that can continually track the enemy, the need for large forces to fix the opposition physically will be less important. . . .
>
> I see battlefields or combat areas that are under 24 hour real or near real time surveillance of all types.
>
> I see battlefields on which we can destroy anything we locate through instant communications and the almost instantaneous application of highly lethal firepower. . . .
>
> Hundreds of years were required to achieve the mobility of the armored division. A little over two decades later we had the airmobile division. With cooperative effort, no more than ten years should separate us from the [completely] automated battlefield.[17]

The enthusiasm for automated killing evidenced in such utterances is not shared by everyone. The specter of increasingly technologized, impersonal, indiscriminate violence as "the wave of the future" is one that causes many men to question seriously the kind of mentality and society that it is in the process of creating. The following words are taken from testimony by Eric Herter before the "Winter Soldier" Investigation of the Air War, 1971:

> This new war will not produce My Lais. . . . It will be a war not of men at arms, but of computers and weapons systems against whole populations. Even the tortured bond of humanity between enemies at war will be eliminated.
>
> Under its auspices, the people of the villages have gone from being "gooks" and "dinks" to being grid-coordinates, blips on scan screens, dots of light on infrared film. They are never seen, never known, never even hated. The machine functions, the radar blip disappears. No village is destroyed, no humans die. For none existed.
>
> It is hard to feel responsible for this type of war, even for those who were close to it. There is little personal involvement. The atrocity is the result of a chain of events in which no man plays a single decisive part.
>
> The technicians who program the computer perform no act of war, the man who places the sensor does not see it operate. The man who plots the strike never sees the plane that conducts it. The pilot, navigator, and bombardier do not see the bomb hit. The damage assessor was not in the plane, and all the others who helped mount the raid never participated in it at all.
>
> We are not really sanguine about this. We know the American public has a large capacity for forgetting what it does not care to remember. New sensations will catch the general fancy . . . while a perpetual electronic war is perfected in Indochina.[18]

A society able to conduct such mindless, indiscriminate violence against a helpless agricultural populace might seem on the surface to be a society quite stripped of humane impulse. Yet this is not the case. Paradoxically, the steady erosion of moral sensitivity toward mass-killing-at-a-distance has taken place at a time when moral sensitivity in many other departments of life has *increased*. The degradation of warfare since the eighteenth century does not, as Roland Bainton observes, signify a *general* deterioration of Western man:

> On the contrary, the nineteenth and twentieth centuries have seen a great increase in humanitarian feeling manifest in civilian life. The eighteenth century was brutal in its treatment of criminals, underlings, and unfortunates; in its amusements; and in its sports. The modern age spends incredible sums to reclaim the reclaimable and to keep alive the irreclaimable. There has emerged an ever-widening discrepancy between sensitivity in civilian relations and callousness in military behavior.[19]

Among the reasons for this are those connected with the technology of modern war: the kind of killing that technology has made normative today is impersonal, anonymous, dissociated from people, and disconnected from consequences; it therefore tends to elude the moral inhibitions operative under more usual circumstances, and is therefore easier to do. "Offenses that transcend our imagination by virtue of their monstrosity are committed more readily, for the inhibitions normally present when the consequences of a projected action are more or less calculable are no longer operative."[20] Thus, while sensitivity toward people (which means, in part, sensitivity against killing) has generally increased with the progress of civilization, this movement has been overbalanced, in certain crucial areas, by the technologically induced ease with which killing can now be done.

> If moral responsibility and unwillingness to kill have indubitably increased, the ease and emotional impunity of killing have increased at the same rate. The distance at which all shooting weapons take effect screens the killer against the stimulus which would otherwise activate his killing inhibitions. The deep, emotional layers of our personality simply do not register the fact that the crooking of the forefinger to release a shot tears the entrails of another man. No sane man would even go rabbit hunting for pleasure if the necessity of killing his prey with his natural weapons brought home to him the full, emotional realization of what he is actually doing.
>
> The same principle applies, to an even greater degree, to the use of modern, remote-control weapons. The man who presses the releasing button is so completely screened against seeing, hearing, or otherwise emotionally realizing the consequences of his action, that he can commit it with impunity—even if he is burdened with the power of imagination. Only thus can it be explained that perfectly good-natured men, who would not even spank a naughty child, proved to be perfectly able to release rockets or to lay carpets of incendiary bombs on sleeping cities, thereby committing hundreds of thousands of children to a horrible death in the flames. The fact that it is good, normal men who did this is as eerie as any fiendish atrocity of war! [21]

One should therefore not assume that man today is generally less humane or sensitive than formerly; it would be truer to say that even the increasing sensitivity he has is as yet unable to cope with the radical new demands placed upon it by the advent of modern weapons. Technology has outrun the moral sense:

In general we seem to have moved by stages into the position that *anything is permitted at a distance,* while there are still moral limits in the treatment of prisoners or other individuals close at hand. We could shrug off or even sanction the killing of a hundred thousand people, mostly civilians, in a single raid on Dresden or Hamburg or Tokyo, but we still would refrain from sanctioning the torture of one individual whom we could face as a person. There was a deterioration of our moral judgment under the pressure of war. *The technological momentum of weapons outran our moral imagination.* That momentum continues and the pressure of the cold war has kept us from recovering our moral balance.[22]

Bennett's observations in this passage give substance to the now famous cliché that man's technical competence and power have outstripped his existing moral capacities. This is so in the sense that the magnitude of destructive power now accessible to his technical genius far transcends his presently existing imagination, sensitivity, and feelings, both individually and collectively. His capacity to act is virtually infinite; his capacity to imagine, feel, and respond remains limited. Mass extermination is an event so enormous, physically and morally, as to be essentially devoid of appreciable human meaning. It transcends the imagination; as Günther Anders observes, it lies "outside the realm of moral apperception." [23] Its consequences "are so great that the agent cannot possibly grasp them before, during, or after his action." [24] Thus, at last, man is able to *do* that which he cannot possibly *grasp.* It is possible, says Anders, to repent one murder, not a million murders.[25]

This bizarre incongruence between the capacity for action and the capacity for moral apperception turns modern man, as Anders observes, into a kind of "inverted Faust":

Whereas Faust had infinite anticipations and boundless feelings, and suffered because his finite knowledge and power were unequal to these feelings, we know more and produce greater things than we can imagine or feel.[26]

Or, to change the metaphor:

In our emotional responses we remain at the rudimentary stage of small artisans: we are barely able to repent an individual murder; whereas in our capacity for killing, for producing corpses, we have already entered the proud stage of industrial mass production. . . . The gulf between our emotional capacity and our destructive powers, aside from representing a physical threat to our lives, makes us the most divided, the most disproportionate, the most inhuman beings that have ever existed.[27]

It must not be supposed that the limitations discussed above are solely individual. If this were so, we could rest comfortably in the assurance that they would be compensated by the controls and restraints imposed by the institutions of society. But these limitations are not solely individual; they are structural, social, institutional.

Institutions and social structures do essentially two things: (1) they expand the powers of the individual, *enabling* him to do things he could not do by himself; and (2) they impose controls and restraints on the individual, *preventing* him from doing things he could do by himself. Modern weapons systems, as a structure, do both of these: (1) By the establishment of complex technical and human controls, they restrain the individual from the commission of unauthorized acts (i.e., they impose upon him a "responsibility" which he may or may not possess personally). (2) Yet, by placing the individual in a context where the potential effect of his decisions and actions is magnified infinitely beyond the scope of his own imagination or sense of personal responsibility, they make possible the very failure of responsibility that their controls are designed to forestall.

Thus, the limitations of responsibility and imagination are not solely individual; they are systemic. If killing in the nuclear age is easier to do than ever before, this is not because there is something wrong with individuals; it is because the weapons systems, for reasons explored earlier, have made it that way. Their very nature is such as to magnify the limitations of the individual and to render those limitations potentially disastrous.

Mass extermination is not something that *individuals* do, in and of themselves; they can effect this result only by acting as part of a total system, which has been expressly devised for the purpose. "The men who carry out such actions are always co-agents: they are either half-active and half-passive cogs in a vast mechanism, or they serve merely to touch off an effect that has been prepared in advance to the extent of 99 per cent." [28] Thus, the really decisive "irresponsibility" is that which characterizes *the system itself*, as a total process. The system is programmed for mass extermination; this is its very essence, the only thing it is able to do. If the individual takes part in a sequence whose end product is mass extermination, he is able to do so only because the sequence is already there, programmed into a system whose final intended result is an evil more hideous than could ever be devised, understood, imagined, or felt by any of the participating agents individually.

The ultimate "irresponsibility" is social and political. Mass destruction as a system exploits the limited moral capacities of the individual by separating him from his victims and from the results of his actions, thus making it possible for him to commit hideous destruction with relative emotional ease. Yet mass destruction as a system is a *social* process, existing by dint of *political* decision and enjoying the sanction of society as a whole. It came into being, not solely because individuals have limited moral capacities; it did so because the moral capacities of society itself are defective in the same way. Essentially the man at the bombsight or the nuclear control panel merely reflects the moral dissociation of society as a whole. This dissociation is largely traceable to the nature of modern weapons. It is easy to kill—if the killing is done massively and at great distances. The moral impact of this condition falls not merely upon the immediate "co-agents" of mass destruction; it has modified the moral sensitivity of society as such. What is difficult to *imagine* is easy to *do;* and what is easy to *do* is easy to *accept.* John Bennett's observation that "anything is permitted at a distance" is not a diagnosis of the individual soul; it describes the moral condition of society. Mass destruction is a social institution. The ethic of mass destruction is a social ethic.

This is not to deny that controls exist. There are counterweights built into the system, which serve as sources of "structural responsibility." These include: technical controls; the psychological screening of personnel; the difficulty of any one person, acting alone, to fire a missile; the Washington–Moscow hot line; etc. Nor should one fail to mention the multitude of international institutions and political processes whose effect is to reduce tension, promote understanding, achieve limited agreements, adjudicate disputes, and devise controls that diminish the likelihood of general war. I would not deny the importance of these. Yet it remains terrifyingly obvious that the nuclear machine, as now constituted, has the power to cancel out all these arrangements, to annihilate perhaps totally and forever all the human values which they are designed to protect. Thus one should note the ambivalence of a total situation that seems to pull in both directions at once. Our institutions, our ethics, are both "responsible" and "ir-responsible" at the same time. They protect us from danger, but the danger they protect us from is the very danger they themselves have done so much to create and to magnify. Clearly, such "protection" cannot protect for-ever.

We face a world today in which the issue of "responsi-bility" is posed with a new and desperate urgency. Vastly increased numbers of men have become decision makers; the power of technology has enormously extended the im-pact of those decisions, and immensely expanded the num-bers of human lives upon which the impact falls. This process has been going on since the beginning of the in-dustrial revolution; now, at last, with the introduction of potentially "total" weapons, the process has reached a kind of end point: we are now able to make decisions whose im-pact extends around the entire planet and falls with po-tentially irreversible finality upon every living creature in existence. The Bible tells us to subdue and have dominion over the earth (Gen., ch. 1). We have done so with a vengeance.

This fact places upon us, at last, a responsibility of truly fearful dimensions. In the "global village" that we have created with our technical genius, every man, every so-ciety, is our "neighbor"; we are accountable to all of them. We ourselves have made it that way—and we shall have to find the capacity, somehow, to understand this fact, and to act accordingly. There is no other option.

# 7.

# THE ANTHROPOLOGY
# OF TECHNICIZED "AGGRESSION"

THE PROBLEM OF "RESPONSIBILITY" CANNOT BE FULLY ANA-
lyzed without an exploration of the problem of "aggression"—a subject that has received increasing attention
during recent years, especially in the literature of anthropology. Responsibility, in one sense, means control; and
one of the major human factors demanding control is aggression. Given the age-old human propensity toward
violence and destructiveness, aggression has always been
a problematic factor in the human economy. In the nuclear age, this stubbornly persistent reality, technologized
and abstracted, has become a crucial factor in a dangerous
and potentially fatal equation.

Like other persistent human realities, aggression is am-
biguous, complex, multidimensional. For this reason it remains one of those fascinatingly open questions to which
scientists, philosophers, and theologians perennially return for new probings.

I shall not be concerned here to determine what aggression really is. Such a concern implies the assumption that
there is a necessary cosmic connection between the word
"aggression" and some particular category of behavior. Aggression is a concept which may be more or less useful in

designating certain behaviors. The crucial questions are: Does it grasp the "inner logic" of the realities designated? Does it reveal essential dimensions of these realities which would otherwise remain unperceived?

A few writers (e.g., Lorenz, Ardrey) have argued that human aggression, like animal aggression, is instinctive, i.e., that it occurs innately, spontaneously, and in the absence of learning.[1] Most life-scientists, however, reject this notion; they maintain that neither aggression nor any other category of human behavior is instinctive—all are *learned*.[2] Man, it is claimed, has no discoverable instincts: what the lower animals do automatically, by genetic determination, man has to learn to do.[3] Thus, in the transition from pre-man to man, phylogenetic evolution is seen as giving way to "cultural" evolution: the "wisdom" of the genes has been replaced by the consciously devised wisdom of the human brain.

In this respect, man was liberated to some extent from the tyranny of his biological past; he was made free to shape his own future—to bring into existence new structures of being and value not predetermined by the logic and structures of the past. At the same time, his life was rendered much more unstable and problematic, since the indeterminateness of human nature thereafter provided almost unlimited possibility for mischief. Doubtless this is the reason why the history of man has been crammed with viciousness and folly so far beyond the scope of anything the animal world can boast of. From this perspective, one does not need to resort to theories of instinctive aggression to explain the evil in man. It is sufficient to recognize that a creature without instincts is a creature without built-in controls—a creature in whom practically "anything is possible." Some such recognition as this seems to be implicit

in the Genesis mythology: A creature who thinks he can
storm the gates of heaven is a creature whose "trespasses"
stem not from predetermined patterns but from their *absence.* He is a creature whose nature it is constantly *"to
overstep the boundaries."* This is both his glory and his
tragedy.

Those who defend the traditional position that man is
without instincts do not suggest that the psychic energy
which comprises aggression must be thought of as non-
existent until aggressive behavior appears. Aggression is
sometimes defined as a "drive" like hunger and sex. It is
thought to be innately present in the organism, but the
stimuli that release it, the manner of its release, the methods of its control, and its perceived "meaning" in the total
social configuration are determined by cultural and social
factors. They are *learned,* and therefore to some extent
are determinable and modifiable by conscious human
choice.

For the purposes of this chapter, I shall define aggression as behavior whose goal is the injury of some person
or object.[4] In this sense, aggression is essentially synon-
ymous with violence, or a disposition toward violence.
Any form of behavior directed against persons or objects
with the intention of repelling, injuring, or destroying
them may be classed as aggression.

It is tempting to identify aggression as "evil"; those who
do so tend to assume that the essential human task, ethically conceived, is to banish aggression from the human
economy. But the issue is not that simple. Most life-scientists believe that nothing is retained in the march of
evolution which is not of some basic value to the species
in its efforts to survive and flourish. According to the principle of "natural selection," animals having characteristics

with positive survival-value tend to survive and reproduce their kind; those having characteristics with negative survival-value tend not to survive and reproduce. Over long periods, this process eventuates in the improvement or strengthening of a species. We can only assume, in consequence, that aggression has had some degree of survival-value; otherwise *homo sapiens* would not now exist as a species.[5]

The world in which man emerged must have demanded a high expertise in the ways of violence. If man were to get his dinner, and escape to hunt again another day, he would have to be a good fighter. Unlike the other animals, he had neither strength nor speed nor "natural" weapons; he had only his hands, his bigger brain, and such artificial weapons as he could devise. He became a new kind of fighter. For hundreds of thousands of years, he developed and perfected the techniques of violence—and for this reason he survived.

It must be noted that aggression has a value for all animals, quite apart from the problems of food-gathering and self-defense. Life-scientists are agreed that all animals possess some level of spontaneous (instinctive) aggression, which serves a number of useful purposes. Among these are: spacing of individuals over the available "territory," thus ensuring adequate food supply; selecting better-qualified males for breeding through competition; and in social animals, providing leadership and discipline through the formation of an order of dominance ("pecking order"), which allows those with superior "wisdom," experience, strength, and courage to emerge to the advantage of the entire community.

This function of aggression is "preservation." Its purpose is not to destroy animals, but to keep them properly spaced and properly related. If this function is to be successfully maintained, it is obviously essential that the aggression-response be subjected to some instinctive mechanism of control. This, in fact, is precisely the case. The carnivores, which kill members of other species for their food, have, through natural selection, developed powerful inhibiting mechanisms against killing members of their own species. The "most bloodthirsty predators . . . are among the animals with the most reliable killing inhibitions in the world." [6] Although some lethal combat does take place, combat between members of the same species is designed, not to kill, but to establish territorial, sexual, or hierarchical dominance; hence, it is sufficient merely to drive the opponent away or forcibly to establish its place in the "pecking order." Intraspecific aggression tends to become partly ritualized. A gesture of submission by one animal almost always releases an inhibiting mechanism in the other which effectively *prevents* it from doing serious injury to its opponent. The "purpose" of this mechanism is obvious: without it, the carnivores would have annihilated one another long since, and they would all now be extinct.

> A raven can peck out the eye of another with one thrust of its beak, a wolf can rip the jugular vein of another with a single bite. There would be no more ravens and no more wolves if reliable inhibitions did not prevent such actions.[7]

It is also to be noted that the more or less "harmless" animals—the ones that lack real killing power—do not possess this inhibiting mechanism. Natural selection has not developed it, because for the most part it is not needed. The "harmless" animals are no less innately aggressive than the others, but they cannot do the damage that the others can do; hence, no killing inhibitions are necessary.

If rabbits or doves, for example, get into a fight and cannot escape, as in a cage, they may continue to attack one another, without inhibition, until one is killed.

At this point, we begin to confront the human problem. For among the creatures whose aggression is not controlled by any instinctively inhibiting mechanism is man. The reason for this is not hard to determine: physically speaking, man is one of the "harmless" animals. Unlike the carnivores, he lacks "natural" weapons; he has neither strength nor speed nor beak nor claws nor fighting teeth. Consequently, he also lacks the built-in safety devices that inhibit the carnivores from attacking and killing their own kind.

> Better armed animals are better protected by inhibitions against intraspecific aggression; and if men had tusks or horns they would be less, rather than more, likely to kill one another. The artificial weapon is too cerebral a device for nature to have provided adequate safeguards against it.[8]

This is precisely the point at which the problem confronts us, for the discovery of "artificial" weapons quite suddenly provided man with a new killing-power against which nature had developed no instinctive means of restraint. The "invention of artificial weapons upset the equilibrium of killing potential and social inhibition." [9] Or, as Jerome Frank observes, "When we invented weapons, we took evolution by surprise." [10]

Thus, the situation of modern man may be summarized as follows: (1) Without "natural" weapons, and without instincts generally, man has developed no instinctive inhibitions against killing other men; yet his discovery of "artificial" weapons makes him an infinitely more dangerous killer than the most powerful carnivore that ever lived. Hence, as it turns out, man is virtually the only existing creature that systematically and organizedly slaughters other members of its own species. Other known species that do this are rats and ants. (2) "Artificial" weapons, unlike "natural" weapons, are "detachable"; they are not a part of the human organism. They stand apart from man himself, as a product of his technical capacity. Hence, their nature and scope are not "fixed." They are open-ended; there are quite literally no limits to their potential destructiveness. *If limits are to be imposed, they will have to be imposed only by the conscious decision of men, rooted in moral-social inhibitions which, not themselves "given" by nature, must be learned.* Yet the learning of moral inhibitions in this area appears difficult at best. Such inhibitions as do function are not very effective—essentially because they are continually sabotaged by other learned values that contradict them: notably, the honor and excellence of organized killing as a patriotic duty of all good citizens. It is likely that this particular piece of learning will persist until the present system of completely autonomous national states is replaced by some other institution directing the sensitivities of men toward some broader definition of loyalty. The "brotherhood of man" will not really function as an operative value in human affairs until it is given some more satisfactory institutional embodiment than it has now. (3) The learning of new moral inhibitions regarding the use of weapons is made difficult by the escalatory character of technology. Artificial weapons develop so rapidly in complexity and power that by the time inhibitions or controls appropriate to one level have been formed, they are rendered obsolete by the movement of technology to higher levels of destructiveness.[11] As noted in the previous chapter, weapons technology tends to outrun the moral imagination.

We have said that the combat of dangerously armed animals tends to be partly ritualized—seeking not destruction but dominance. Gestures of submission, or "surrender signals" so called, activate inhibitions that prevent the imposition of serious injury or death. It should be especially observed that this dynamic has analogues on the human level. In human situations of combat, surrender signals are often taken as mandatory indications that the combat should stop. Both individual and collective combat involve implicit or explicit "rules," whereby it is generally regarded as morally abhorrent to continue attacking after surrender signals are received. This tendency may be seen as one instance in which human beings (sometimes) achieve through learning what the other animals achieve by instinct.

This pattern will occur, if at all, only if the surrender signals that are sent are also *received*—or received *in time*. This is one major point at which the use of modern weapons becomes problematic. According to one observer:

> Other animals give signals of submission when they are beaten, but man's modern weapons let him kill at a distance and speed that make such signals useless. Insulated from torn flesh, we do not even respond to the pain we cause.[12]

This may overstate the case, but it makes a point nevertheless, as the following extrapolations will show. (1) Because modern weapons kill at great distances, in many cases there is no means of communication between the combatants. It is impossible to surrender while being bombed; no one is listening. (2) Because modern weapons operate at immense speeds, communication between combatants is often too slow to make any difference. A surrender signal received after the missiles had been launched could not make them turn around. Furthermore, how could the receiving side know that the signal was genuine? By the time it had been checked and counterchecked, the missiles would have landed, and those who had sent the signals would have ceased to exist. By that time, their own missiles would doubtless be in flight, and any surrender signals by the other side would be directed at dead men. (3) Because modern weapons require, for their proper control, extremely rapid, accurate communication, especially between combatants or potential combatants, even the slightest garbling of the message could have potentially catastrophic results. Misreading of instruments, misinterpretation of data, misunderstanding of the enemy's words, actions, or intent—all represent points of possible communication breakdown. This limitation would be immensely aggravated by the incredible chaos which even a low-level nuclear conflict would bring about. Under such conditions, it is likely that surrender signals, like most other signals, would simply get lost in "the fury and fog of war."

These considerations pose a serious challenge to those who believe that the practice of nonviolent defense offers a viable answer to the danger of war in the nuclear age. The practice of nonviolent resistance is devised strictly for situations of direct, personal confrontation. It depends for its effectiveness upon transmitting unmistakable signals from the resister to the aggressor expressing, in this case, not surrender but a kind of nonhostile defiance. As one of its foremost proponents has written:

> Non-violent resistance is a means of communicating feelings and ideas. It uses facial expressions, bodily gestures

and tone of voice, just as in all personal communication. In prolonged situations it may also use writing and printing. Its means of expression are as ample as those of any language. Even in situations where words can be used little or not at all, conduct . . . itself may be a rapid, accurate, and efficient means of communication.[13]

Clearly, if nonviolent resistance is a form of communication, it can work only if the persons involved are in a position to receive each other's "messages." It is precisely this factor which is sabotaged by the nature of modern weapons. The two most problematic elements in the equation are speed and distance. If the hand is quicker than the eye, it is no less true that the trigger finger is quicker than the tongue. It may be possible (though, I should think, extremely difficult) to communicate nonviolently while being beaten; it is clearly impossible to do so while being *shot*. And it must be even more difficult to communicate in this fashion—or in any fashion—with an opponent who is too far away to be listening. Clearly, nonviolent defense is no answer to *this* problem.

There are two ways in which aggression may be "technologized." (1) One is a kind of "sublimation." By this means, the individual feeds his destructive energies into a machine process which is itself not destructive but creative: i.e., it is programmed to produce a product (e.g., refrigerators) which is not itself an instrument of aggression. As the destructive energies are mediated through the machine, they become creative because they are subsumed by a mechanical process that has been pre-set to produce a "good" end product regardless of the motives of those who run the machine. (2) The second way is by "delegation." By this means the individual mediates his destructive energies through a machine (i.e., a weapon) which is itself programmed as an instrument of destruction. In this case, one may say, the individual has delegated his aggression to a machine; he "touches off" the machine by pulling the trigger or pressing the button, but the machine itself commits the act of destruction.

What we have here called "delegated" aggression has two crucial characteristics. (a) Its power is immensely magnified by the machine. (b) Because the input required to produce this magnified result is so small, and because the destruction is done indirectly (i.e., by the machine and not by the person), "delegated" aggression is unsatisfying; hence, it tends to be repeated and to escalate.[14]

Direct aggression is clearly more "satisfying" than aggression that is mediated through a weapon. A man equipped with a weapon is likely to achieve a much higher level of destruction on the strength of a much lower level of personal aggression than a man without one. The fury of a Charles Whitman, exercised directly (i.e., without a weapon), would surely have led to great personal violence, possibly even to murder; mediated through a rifle, and at great distance from the victims, it led to *mass* murder. *One* victim was not sufficient; it was too easy. Pulling a trigger is not a satisfactory means of dissipating aggression. It requires too little effort, and the destruction is performed by a machine and not by oneself. In order to dissipate the personal aggression that is present, one must fire again and again, thus multiplying the level of destruction beyond all proportion to its cause. Thus, as noted, "delegated" aggression tends to be repeated and to escalate.[15]

At the level of nuclear weapons, the disproportion is virtually infinite. A person could, we suppose, press the fatal switch that would exterminate several million people *without dissipating his personal aggression in the slightest.*

Yet, since the degree of aggression required to *motivate* pressing that switch is extremely small, or practically non-existent, it is easy to assume that those who man the weapons systems are faced from time to time with a serious temptation to do so. One can only hope that "Smith" and "Jones" (see above, p. 87) do not both get this temptation at the same time.

## 8.

## UNINTENDED WAR:
## THE PRESUMPTION
## OF PERFECT CONTROL

IN THE TWO PRECEDING CHAPTERS WE HAVE ANALYZED FACtors that increase the possibility of a nuclear exchange. In Chapter 6 we noted that mass destruction, for several reasons, is dangerously easy to initiate. In Chapter 7 we noted that man, having no instinctive inhibitions against killing (including mass killing), is restrained from such excesses only by consciously contrived inhibitions, which are dangerously unreliable. These two factors represent points at which technology and the nature of man come together in such a way as to increase the likelihood of a catastrophe that nobody actually wants. Thus, the tragedy of nuclear weapons is that they make highly possible a disaster which from the standpoint of the ultimate hopes and intentions of men is essentially *accidental*. In the present chapter, we shall explore other factors that enhance this possibility.

The problem of unintended war relates essentially to two issues: (1) the control of violence already initiated, and (2) the prevention of violence that one does not wish to initiate in the first place. In the first instance, the objective is to ensure that violence already initiated does not elude control and escalate to unintended levels. In the second instance, the objective is to ensure that unintended violence does not accidentally *begin*. The first objective has to do with keeping a "limited" nuclear war limited; the second has to do with keeping nuclear weapons inert— safeguarding against their "unintended" use. These two objectives are highly problematical, because each relies, in its own way, on what I call "the presumption of perfect control"—a presumption that, under conditions of human fallibility and finitude, is an illusion. Given the nature of nuclear weapons, it is the ultimate illusion.

## I. Limited War:
### The Illusion of Perfect Rationality

As indicated in Chapter 4, the United States has toyed, since the late 1950's, with the notion of "tactical" nuclear war. Such "limited" war, as I pointed out, would be little more than an exercise in near-total devastation. One reason is the magnitude of even "small" nuclear weapons; an equally important reason is the tendency of nuclear weapons to resist control: that is, the magnitude of the weaponry brought to bear in any serious encounter escalates.

"Conventional" weapons, based on chemical explosives, have a built-in limitation; the ratio of weight to firepower is such that weapons beyond a certain level of destructiveness are simply too heavy to manage. Ten tons is about the maximum so far achieved. Thus, conventional weapons are incapable of escalation beyond a certain point. (Even that point is pretty high: ask the people of Indochina.) This is not true of nuclear weapons. In this case, the ratio of weight to firepower makes virtually unlimited destructiveness possible. Nuclear power contains no built-in limitations; *the only limitations available must be those imposed by human choice—a highly unreliable agency.* Thus it seems likely, in the event of "tactical" nuclear war, that the participant powers, having serious objectives at stake and lacking any inherent cutoff point, would tend to recoup each military setback by escalating their own firepower one more "notch," believing each time that the present notch would be the last:

> Once the threshold of atomic weaponry is crossed in battle, the pressure for use of "just one higher level" of atomic force will be practically irresistible. The side badly hurt by atomic artillery shells will respond by dropping medium-sized atomic bombs on the offending artillery emplacements. The answer to that will be larger bombs or medium-range missiles against the airfields from which the tactical atomic strikes had come. Quickly the side less equipped with tactical nuclear weapons . . . will feel pressed to resort to thermo-nuclear attack. The ladder to disaster will be quickly climbed if the phantom of "high firepower tactical strength" is pursued by the West.[1]

Advocates of tactical nuclear war tend to deny the essentially escalatory character of such warfare by appeal to the notion of human rationality. Man, they observe, is a rational being—capable of self-control. There is no inexorable logic which compels man to do that which he does not will to do. Thus, in the words of Thomas E. Murray, already quoted as an advocate of tactical nuclear war:

> There is, of course, always the possibility of an extension to all-out war. One would be foolish to deny it. But to insist that hostilities which began as limited in scope would inevitably set off a chain reaction culminating in all-out nuclear war is to admit that man cannot control his own actions and choices.[2]

Likewise, in a magazine article some years ago, Murray expressly denied that:

> any use of nuclear weapons inevitably means the totalization of the conflict. This is not true. A nuclear war can still be a limited war. To believe otherwise is to deny that man is a rational being capable of controlling his own actions.[3]

Murray obviously believes that man *is* "a rational being capable of controlling his own actions." I regret that I cannot share this sublime confidence in the power of human rationality. Surely it is true that man is capable of self-control—*partially*. His self-control, I should say, is seriously compromised, both by internal weaknesses and by the impact of processes which, though initiated by human decision, yet tend to function thereafter as autonomous determinants of behavior. If anything I have said so far in this book is valid, its ultimate effect is to show that all such claims for human rationality are sheer fantasy. How *fragile* human rationality is—how easily subject to unconscious distortion by factors that modify perception without its "consent."

1. To say that man is always capable of self-control is to say that man always does what he wills to do. Yet even if this were true (and I believe that it is not), the *basic* problem has not even been touched: the fact that man, for reasons beyond his understanding and control, very often "wills" to do that which is evil, stupid, and self-defeating.[4] Most men doubtless agree that all-out nuclear war would be calamitous; yet this fact in itself clearly offers *no assurance whatever* that such an event would not occur. Under conditions of any nuclear war, escalation clearly

could take place, and if it did, it would do so because men, under those conditions, had so decided. ("Sin," as Christianity has always insisted, is a matter of "will.")

2. Even at that, man does not always do what he "wills" to do. He is *not* always "in control." Events get out of hand; under the pressure of ignorance, misinformation, confusion, hatred, or panic, he reacts blindly and precipitately, thereby initiating processes that increasingly remove the situation from rational human control. It seems almost certain, indeed, that such conditions would obtain during even the most "limited" nuclear war:

> Battles are still fought by men, and in the heat of battle their behavior is not altogether subject to rigid control. How will they act in the utter confusion of a nuclear engagement, with whole battalions wiped out at a blow, communications destroyed, and officers in the dark about how the battle is going? What sort of chain of command can be established? Who will have the ultimate say on what weapons are fired? Above all, how will the battle be ended? Will either side accept defeat, so long as it still has powerful weapons that can be thrown into the balance, limited war or no limited war? To suggest that nuclear conflict could be disciplined or restrained from expanding is indeed an armchair exercise.[5]

As noted in Chapter 4, violence, with or without weapons of mass destruction, tends to elude rational control. It tends to be self-reinforcing. This is so because violence is itself essentially nonrational: it involves powerful emotions (hatred, fear, panic, etc.) and it introduces chaotic elements into the environment, both of which resist control. Violence involves the destruction of order, which is the system of limitations, self-imposed or collectively imposed, governing human behavior. For this reason, it tends to spill over the boundaries originally intended to contain it. One speaks of violence "breaking out," thus expressing the loss of rational control that is often involved. What is sometimes overlooked is that the intentional, calculated violence brought to bear *against* the outbreak (and the violence of organized warfare is of this type) is itself subject to the same tendency.[6] The rational determination to avoid excess is no guarantee against it. This is so because the use of violence produces, in the user and in the victim alike, an emotional state which tends to destroy rational self-control. Once this happens, violence tends to escalate, and to resist efforts to terminate it.

These characteristics, intrinsic to violence as such, would be magnified to the nth degree under conditions even of "limited" nuclear war. One can scarcely imagine the chaos, confusion, and large-scale emotional traumatizing that the conduct of such an engagement would produce. To speak of "rational control" under such conditions is to indulge in the sheerest fantasy. At best, man is only a partially rational being; under conditions of nuclear war, even such rationality as he possesses would surely be the first major casualty. Escalation would be the order of the day.

I would venture to suggest that the overconfidence in human reason is an expression of what is often called the sin of pride—a sin that modern man, unduly impressed with his own omnicompetence, possesses in marvelous abundance. As one writer has put it:

We have been trapped, trapped by our egos, into believing that under any conditions we human beings can control both ourselves and the limitless machines to which we attach ourselves. This belief grew out of 17th-century rationalism, and has been reinforced by our spectacular success in mastering our environment. And we *are* good—

> damned good [an expletive perhaps with theological sig-
> nificance]—at creating a world in our image and in
> controlling that world. But there are little foxes, fragile
> seams, weak links, Achilles' heels, endemic to the human
> condition.[7]

We might be well advised to take these limitations into
account in our estimate of man in the nuclear age. Otherwise they could prove fatal.


## II. Accidental War:
### Supertechnology, Finitude, and Stress

All weapons—in fact, all machines—are subject to accident. This is so simply because the condition of finitude
imposes limitations upon all things. It is impossible to con-
struct a machine or a system of machines that will not,
sometime, break down. It is equally impossible to find human beings who are not subject, at some level, to errors of
judgment, not to say irrationality. These factors, as noted,
are universally applicable; they are no less applicable to
weapons of mass destruction and to the men who monitor
them.

The more complex a machine or a system becomes, the
more delicate is the internal balance, the interrelation
among parts, required to keep it properly functioning.
Each part represents a point of potential breakdown;
hence the more parts a machine has, the more vulnerable to
malfunction it becomes. Moreover, as the parts increase in
number, the total number of interrelationships among
them increases exponentially; hence the internal balance
becomes more and more fragile.

Nuclear weapons systems are the most complex mechanisms ever devised by man. A single malfunction in any

one of these systems could mean one of two things: (1) the machine would fail to work; (2) the machine would work in some "unintended" or "unauthorized" way. The first of these might be merely inconvenient; the second could be catastrophic.

In his book *The Peace Race*, Seymour Melman discussed the possibility of machine malfunction:

> Columbia University has 1,419 telephones on Morningside Heights, New York City, located in closed, well-protected premises, which are not normally subjected to heavy physical use. The operation of this system requires the full-time attendance of a telephone company maintenance man— and this is a relatively small communications network. When even simple electrical systems, operating under sheltered conditions, are subject to continuous failure, we must realize and accept the constant threat from failure of complex control mechanisms of atomic weapons.[8]

American nuclear weapons are loaded with safety devices, and their maintenance is subject to the most rigid restrictions; hence the danger of accident at any given time is extremely small. Nevertheless, the very operability of the weapons imposes a limiting factor on safety. "Since the safeguards cannot be so elaborate that they interfere with intentional firing, there is an upper limit to the protection they can afford."[9]

Proliferation of *parts* increases the danger of accident; proliferation of *weapons* does the same. Each weapon represents a potential accident; hence every increase in the number of existing weapons represents an increase in the number of possible accidents. This factor is immensely enhanced by the increasing numbers of personnel required to man and service this expanding arsenal. "As large numbers of fast-flying missiles come into the possession of both sides, ready for use, critical command will tend to de-volve to lower and lower echelons." [10] This is so because missile crews must be—and are—at least partially autono-mous. They must be free to act on their own judgment in the event that higher-command centers have been de-stroyed. They must be free, that is, to fire the missiles on their own authority if necessary, even in the absence of directives from above. This proliferation of authority repre-sents a serious attenuation of control, and must be seen as a factor tending to increase the danger of war by accident.

The magnitude of the risk may perhaps be appreciated by reference to the magnitude of the arsenal itself. As of August 1972, the United States and Soviet Russia pos-sessed, according to various estimates, from 8,100 to 8,200 warheads between them (U.S. total: 5,700 to 5,900; Soviet total: 2,200 to 2,500). By 1977, it is estimated that this total will have risen to between 13,600 and 14,000 (U.S. total: 10,000 to 11,000; Soviet total: 2,600 to 4,000).[11] It is difficult to calculate how many tens of thousands of per-sonnel now have, or will increasingly have, access to these weapons. No matter how rigid the controls, the sheer mag-nitude of the force must introduce a risk factor of some dimensions.

This danger is doubtless magnified by the eventual spread of nuclear weapons to other nations. Safety precau-tions in the United States are highly developed. They may or may not be comparable to those in the Soviet Union or in the People's Republic of China. It is logical to suppose, indeed, that nations less highly organized and less tech-nologically sophisticated will be unable and/or unwilling to provide the level of control available to the great powers.

The spread of nuclear weapons to less sophisticated and

perhaps less responsible nations not now possessing them does not represent an immediate danger. It is unlikely that any of these nations will ever be a direct military threat either to the United States or to the Soviet Union. Nevertheless, small nations (many of which represent points of conflict between the United States and the Soviet Union) may use nuclear weapons on each other, thereby not only doing immense damage to themselves but also drawing the great powers into a possible nuclear confrontation where the stakes are too high to permit "backing down."

This could happen, for example, in the seemingly endless Arab-Israeli conflict. As of this writing, the two sides are observing a precarious cease-fire following their most recent war. The cautious restraint displayed by the United States and the Soviet Union in this affair is commendable, not to say momentarily reassuring. Nevertheless, there is little to make anyone suppose that what is merely the latest in a long series of Arab-Israeli wars will not be followed by similar, and possibly more dangerous, conflicts in the future—especially if any of the parties to the conflict get their hands on some form of even "small" (i.e., "tactical") atomic weaponry. At this point, neither side appears willing to modify positions which have, in the course of more than two decades, taken on the character of religiopolitical dogmas. And, in *their* turn, the United States and the Soviet Union, whatever they may say to each other privately, remain publicly and officially committed to seeing their own respective client states prevail. It is not likely that either the United States or Soviet Russia would permit any radical upset in the prevailing power relations vis-à-vis the Israelis and the Arabs. It is of materials such as this that potential nuclear confrontations are made.

As noted in the preceding chapter, the necessity for extremely rapid and accurate decision-making, especially under conditions of crisis, substantially increases the risk of potentially disastrous errors of judgment. Nuclear weapons, by their very nature, introduce the possibility of nearly instantaneous warfare. This fact reduces the time span during which crucial decisions must be made. It makes speed and accuracy of judgment essential; at the same time it also makes them more difficult to attain. This would be especially true in time of international crisis, in which decision makers, anxious, exhausted, distrustful, and panicky, would tend to place upon the adversary's behavior the most ominous interpretation.

At this point, we have moved from the "technical" to the "human" dimension. Nuclear weapons systems are a combination of machines and men. Both are fallible. Both are subject to malfunction. At one level of risk, we are faced with the certainty that all men, even the most wise, are subject to errors of judgment. This rather ordinary fact assumes an ominous significance in the context of nuclear weaponry, where every such error is potentially disastrous.

There is probably some danger from the seriously psychotic or psychopathic individual, though this danger is so minute as to be almost negligible, since such individuals are usually detected by screening processes. More serious is the danger posed by two other types of persons: (1) "The apparently normal people who delight in destruction or who are extremely hostile and suspicious. Many of these are experts at concealing their feelings and plans, and no brief screening method can detect them." [12] (2) The second category would include practically everybody, including the fully "normal" person. Every individual, however strong, has a finite stress tolerance. If he is subjected to stress beyond that point, he will break down. Moreover, nearly every person has particular "weak points" that are not ordinarily detectable, simply because (intentionally or not) he avoids those situations in which his weak points become problematic:

> [T]he important psychological predispositions to "operational fatigue" are usually latent and therefore difficult to detect until they are uncovered by catastrophic events. It must be concluded that for the vast majority *the only test for endurance of combat is combat itself.*[13]

The ultimate implication of this fact is that every single person, however "normal," who handles nuclear weapons, represents a potential accident.

The screening programs currently employed by the armed services doubtless greatly minimize the danger of war by human failure. Yet even the best programs are likely to miss (1) the skillful dissembler, and (2) the "normal" person with a low stress-tolerance under particular conditions. Thus in a study of accidental war possibilities, twelve psychiatrists with military experience concluded that "no existing tests will reliably screen out individuals susceptible to mental breakdowns."[14] Likewise, one of the Air Force's own publications admits: "Unauthorized destructive acts cannot be completely prevented."[15] It is disconcerting to consider that "unauthorized destructive acts" might well include the firing of a thermonuclear missile.

Perhaps the factor most crucially relevant to the danger of accidental war is the nature of stress itself—especially stress in the nuclear age and its relationship to inherited patterns of response. The organismic response to threat, as most people know, is one that involves heightened physical readiness but lowered "intellectual" efficiency.[16] In the long view of evolution, this type of response has been adaptive. Under less complex conditions of life, the type of danger most frequently encountered was such as to demand a high level of physical responsiveness. The physiological components of such responsiveness, though temporarily erosive of "intellectual" discrimination, were nevertheless not problematic, because under such conditions the exercise of high-level intellectual discrimination was generally not necessary.

But under conditions of increasing complexity, the nature of crisis radically alters, thereby calling for a new type of responsiveness. Immediate physical dangers, demanding gross physical reaction, increasingly give way to more abstract, remote, intangible ones, demanding refined, "intellectual" judgments.

Yet the problem lies precisely here. It lies in the fact that man is now "forbidden" to do, under stress, precisely what his physiological structure tries to *compel* him to do. He is increasingly called upon to render careful judgments; yet his organism, conditioned by its own age-old, inherited structures, acts in such a way as to sabotage these very attempts. The nature of "stress" has changed; the human organism has not.

Those who man the nuclear weapons systems, or who otherwise find themselves responsible for making rapid and fateful decisions in the nuclear age, confront precisely this kind of situation. They "must carry great responsibility under periods of boredom, interrupted by periods of great tension." [17] Facing the instruments of detection and retaliation, they are presented with a continuing array of "signals" which they must properly interpret. They must remain "intellectually" alert during long periods of forced inactivity and boredom, interspersed by simulated launching drills, or by conditions of extreme crisis, during which they may be called upon to make decisions affecting the very destiny of mankind.

The danger exerted from forced inaction under crisis is complicated by the organismic tension associated with unexpressed anxiety or anger. The "normal" response to stress prepares the organism for exertion—violent action. Yet in this context no action is possible. The source of threat is abstract, intangible; it cannot be physically assaulted. Hence, there is nothing to do. There is no "outlet"—except the nuclear trigger itself. The danger is well expressed by the following observations:

> Coupling the individual human being with the power of the suns has meant that man's physiological response to crisis may no longer be functional—it may be a tragic flaw. He has become an unwilling victim of his own clever machinations. Now that we have attached our brains to intricate machines of near limitless power, and swaddled our tumescent bodies in frustrating physical inaction, even in the thick of warfare, man may become a self-destroying misfit.[18]

In summary, one may say that two basic factors are relevant to the problem of war by accident. One is the demand for a totally infallible system of controls. Given the magnitude of our weapons as they now exist, a serious malfunction would be disaster unparalleled. When even a single mistake is measured potentially by millions of lives, that single mistake is one mistake too many. The prospect of three or four megatons exploding by "accident" over a major city is a prospect we simply cannot allow, excluding the possibility of escalation which such an accident would entail.

The second factor defines the impossibility of ever achieving the first. It is the condition of finitude. Finitude, as noted, imposes limitations upon all things. Men, machines, and systems always break down eventually if they are not first replaced. This rule may be taken as absolute: it is stamped indelibly into the nature and destiny of all created things. It imposes a logic from which there is no exemption. It is a logic which denies that any combination of fallible machines and fallible men, however well-trained or sophisticated, can function into the indefinite future without, at some point, making a mistake. This is true despite the periodic dismantling of old weapons systems and their replacement by new, more sophisticated ones. Such a practice minimizes the probability that weapons systems will malfunction through parts wearing out; but it increases the probability that they will do so because of their continually increasing complexity as well as their continuing proliferation. This probability has been granted even by Herman Kahn, who made the following admission:

> It is difficult to believe that under these circumstances [i.e., of proliferation] an occasional button will not get pressed. . . . We may just be going to live in a world in which every now and then a city or town is destroyed or damaged as a result of blackmail, unauthorized behavior, or an accident.[19]

It would seem that the only way to avoid this fate is to find some mutually acceptable means of dismantling the nuclear machine, at least as presently constituted. Otherwise, no system of controls, however refined, can do more than postpone the inevitable.

In his book *The Arrogance of Power*, Senator William Fulbright at one point addresses these issues. His words are a fitting conclusion to this chapter.

Neither the government nor the universities are making the best possible use of their intellectual resources to deal with the problems of war and peace in the nuclear age. Both seem by and large to have accepted the idea that the avoidance of nuclear war is a matter of skillful "crisis management," as though the last twenty years have only to be improved upon to get us through the next twenty or a hundred or a thousand years.

The law of averages has already been more than kind to us and we have had some very close calls. . . . None of us, however—professors, bureaucrats, or politicians—has yet undertaken a serious and concerted effort to put the survival of our species on some more solid foundation than an unending series of narrow escapes.[20]

The time for that effort is *now*.

# 9.

## GETTING THE GENIE BACK IN THE BOTTLE

THE PURPOSE OF THIS WORK HAS BEEN TO EXPLORE THE IM-
pact of nuclear weapons upon the ways men feel, think,
decide, and act in relation to issues involving the value of
human life and the intentional killing of other men. This
impact dramatizes, in the strongest manner possible, the
terrible ambiguity imposed upon man by his self-chosen
lordship of the planet Earth. We have made ourselves the
masters of Nature—custodians of its ultimate powers. A
godlike status indeed: yet, in assuming it, we have paid a
terrible price, a price that ultimately calls into question our
own continued survival as a species. To appropriate absolute power inescapably contains the threat of self-de-
struction—the absolute *loss* of power. Thus, we ask once
again: Can we get the genie back in the bottle? Are we not,
in a sense, at the mercy of our own ingenuity?

At the end of the story of the Sorcerer's Apprentice, the
old Sorcerer returns and "saves the day" by restoring
control over the forces so brashly released. This conclusion, sad to say, does not reflect the real world. Here, the
only possible control is that which is exercised by man
himself. There is no *deus ex machina* to which we can appeal to save us from our own mistakes. Whatever may be

the ultimate intentions of God for his creation, there is little prospect of a heavenly intervention to reverse the course of the history for which man alone is responsible.

Responsible exercise of control, in my judgment, demands initiatives toward nuclear disarmament, under appropriate international machinery. The issues discussed in previous chapters convince me that nuclear weapons are an evil whose indefinitely continued maintenance is morally intolerable. Because they are, by their very nature, instruments of massive, indiscriminate destruction, their use under any conditions would be a moral atrocity of unspeakable wickedness. Indeed, their very existence falls under the same condemnation, since even to possess them, if long continued, must *lead* to their use, either by accident or by intent.

Nuclear weapons are instruments of genocide. This is intrinsic to their nature: they cannot be used in any other way. No amount of casuistry can alter that fact. The kind of war that nuclear weapons would produce reduces to sophistry any distinctions which purport to show that such an act could in any sense be moral, rational, or politically meaningful. The initiation of nuclear war, for whatever reason, would be the final obscenity, the last madness of a society that had lost not only its moral bearings but its very hold on reality. No discussion of "double effect," "limited war," "counterforce strategy," or whatnot, can change the fact that nuclear war means one thing, and one thing only: *mass murder*.

Our continuing existence under the nuclear umbrella has led to a false sense of security. The short-run success of nuclear weapons in deterring the war in which they would be used has led us to suppose that the same arrangements may be safely relied upon into the indefinite future. I believe that this supposition is seriously mistaken. Even our past "success" has brought us terrifyingly close to failure, and we cannot logically expect it to continue forever. On several occasions during the past two decades, we have come within a hair's breadth of Armageddon, and our escape from the final abyss may perhaps be due more to good luck than to rationality. How long can we reasonably expect such good fortune to continue? To recall the statement of Senator Fulbright, quoted at the end of the preceding chapter, we must make an effort "to put the survival of our species on some more solid foundation than an unending series of narrow escapes."

However, there is no unshakable security, no absolute guarantee, even in a denuclearized world. The threat is inescapably permanent. We must eventually be able to abolish nuclear weapons "before," as John F. Kennedy said, "they abolish us"; but we cannot abolish the knowledge of how to make them. Once a piece of knowledge has become a part of the public domain, its destruction is impossible. This is true of nuclear knowledge. We have it; nothing can reverse that fact. What has been discovered cannot be erased from the mind. Therefore we must accept the fact that the ability to manufacture and to use nuclear weapons cannot be eliminated; they have become indelibly part of the human story. The threat and the challenge are permanent and inescapable; they will be with us as long as the human race endures, even unto the millionth generation if such there be. There is no escaping the burden of ethical responsibility—ever.

Dangerous knowledge cannot—should not—be eliminated; but it *can* be used in more responsible and less dangerous ways. We should not bemoan the knowledge of nuclear power. Such knowledge is evil only if wrongly applied. Its possession makes possible structures of human good hitherto inconceivable. In any case, we are "stuck" with it. The crucial task, therefore, is to embody a knowledge that is dangerous in structures which (1) do not capriciously maximize the danger, (2) do not tend to elude control, and (3) do not systematically corrupt moral sensitivity. These conditions cannot be fulfilled in a world armed with nuclear weapons.

The conflicts that engage the nuclear nations in the world today are real and will doubtless continue, with or without nuclear weapons. Also, the values at stake are serious and cannot be brushed aside lightly. Nevertheless, it is important to put this understanding in perspective. A world entirely dominated by Soviet and Chinese power is not a very engaging prospect;[1] a world in which all the people are dead is an even less engaging one. This does not mean that we need be confronted with a barren choice between being "Red" or "dead." It *does* mean that all the factors in the moral equation should be put in perspective.

To put the issue in perspective is to recognize that most political conflicts, even the most serious, do not last forever and do not possess ultimate importance. Under the pressure of serious conflict, it is temptingly easy to lose perspective and to identify the values, purposes, and objectives then being defended as absolutely decisive for the future of all mankind for all time to come. This idolatry of national values, and its presumption of decisiveness, notably characterizes the "better dead than Red" adherents. They see the alternatives in such stark terms that they are apparently willing not only that they themselves should be dead but that all future generations should likewise be dead, if only the scourge of Communism be halted.[2] People who think of their own purposes in such dogmatic terms are led to defend them with added persistence, ferocity, and ruthlessness. They tend to think of the conflict as a holy crusade, and to reject any resolution of it short of "total victory." Such an orientation is very dangerous in the nuclear age.

Most conflicts do not represent issues of life-and-death importance to mankind. The great conflicts that grip the world in our own day are not, in my judgment, exempt from this general observation. A century from now, Communism and capitalism, as presently understood, will be a matter of history. The great issues that now stir the blood of patriots on either side will be little more than curiosity pieces for the scholar. How foolish and tragic it will have been if the nations, in the spirit of a new holy war, destroy each other, together with all the values they are presuming to defend, for the sake of differences which a century hence would be of little concern to anyone except historians. Herbert Butterfield has said, "With modern weapons we could easily put back civilization a thousand years, while the course of a single century can produce a colossal transition from despotic regimes to a system of liberty." [3] Likewise, John Bennett has denied that Communism is a greater threat to humanity than nuclear war. "Not only is Communism not inherited genetically [like radioactive poisoning]," he observes, "but Communist children like other children already rebel against their parents' absolutisms!" [4] This is, happily, no less true of American children, whose profound disaffection with current American values has been well documented (Keniston, Roszak, Reich, and others); probably the crucial reconciliations will be accomplished by a new generation that has, in large measure, liberated itself from the vicious and stultifying mythologies of the Cold War.

This is not necessarily to be taken as an argument for unilateral nuclear disarmament. Unilateral disarmament is usually taken to mean that the complete process of disarming, from start to finish, is carried out by one side regardless of the other's response at any point. I do not advocate this course of action as a first priority, because I believe that it is unlikely to succeed for a number of reasons:

1. Unilateral nuclear disarmament is not a policy that any existing government, in the light of its perceived responsibilities, can realistically be expected to consider. Those who advocate such a policy are doubtless to some degree effective in "pricking the conscience" of public officials and keeping the moral issues alive; but they must not expect their policy suggestions to be taken seriously.

2. Unilateral disarmament of any kind is so antithetical to the range of policy options available to governments that its adoption, regardless of public insistence, would very likely be interpreted by opponent nations as a trick. Such an assessment would materially increase the danger of "accidental" war.

3. Unilateral nuclear disarmament, precisely because it *is* unilateral, could provide no substitute for the short-run deterrent power of the weapons it had previously utilized for this purpose. Thus its adoption would constitute an immediate invitation to unrestrained assertions of power by the nation or nations that had not disarmed. This would be true no matter which side disarmed. Soviet Russia is not the only power in the world whose grand pretensions need to be "deterred."

4. Neither the United States nor the Soviet Union could adopt a policy of unilateral nuclear disarmament without by that fact publicly adjuring its previously declared re-

sponsibility to deter the exercise of aggression or inter-
ference against its nonnuclear allies.

For these reasons I believe that unilateral nuclear disarmament is not a live option, except as a last resort. Thus
I agree with John Bennett that under present conditions
"there is no way of escaping from the moral burden of
possessing nuclear weapons, of seeking [by their means]
to preserve a precarious balance of power in the world." [5]
Yet I also believe, for reasons which must be obvious by
now, that this arrangement can be no more than a kind
of desperate *interim* policy, to be effective only until such
time as a viable program of multilateral nuclear disarmament, with international controls, has been undertaken.
Such an achievement will surely be a staggeringly difficult
task. But it is, I believe, ultimately the only acceptable option. The present dispensation cannot continue indefinitely.
It is morally corrupting, and it will surely lead, in time, to
nuclear disaster, by accident or by intent. With every
passing year, this eventuality becomes increasingly certain.
The only way to escape it is to take seriously the task of
nuclear disarmament—starting *now*.

Long and frustrating experience has shown that it is
fruitless to anticipate even minimal progress toward
multilateral nuclear disarmament as long as either or both
sides persist in the present method of negotiation, whereby
each concession by one side is made only on condition that
a corresponding and guaranteed concession be granted
by the other. It is possible to negotiate in this fashion unto
the nth generation, without moving a single inch off home
plate. The Strategic Arms Limitation Talks (SALT) are
a case in point. During four years of almost continuous
negotiation, the American position, as Edgar Bottome sug-

gests, has remained the same: *The United States will arm in order to disarm.*

> While the diplomats talked, American MIRVs became operational and the Administration mustered $1.3 billion appropriation through Congress for the expansion of the ABM system. These multibillion-dollar systems were to be the "bargaining chips" at Vienna in negotiations with the Russians.[6]

Clearly, such a position is designed to *preclude* any significant progress toward arms limitation. The continual insistence upon new "bargaining chips" means an escalated arms race even as the talks proceed. Each new "bargaining chip" represents a higher stake. Even if a treaty is achieved whereby some limitations are placed upon that particular "chip," the resultant level of weaponry is no lower, and possibly even higher, than it was prior to the treaty. This is a clear case of making progress by taking "one step forward, two steps backward." Such a procedure will keep the diplomats busy for generations; but it is unlikely to make any significant headway toward the limitation of arms. It is quite literally an assurance that nuclear disarmament will *never* be achieved. Perhaps it is also a convenient means whereby successive administrations committed to maintaining the nuclear establishment at high levels can give the appearance of being disarmament-minded by "going through the motions," in a continuing diplomatic round robin that is finally calculated to change nothing.

There is some indication that even such modest successes as *are* achieved may turn out to be failures in disguise. Mr. Nixon's treaty with the Soviets limiting the number of land-based and sea-based missile launchers, "imposes no curbs whatever on the development of more powerful warheads, the installation of multiple warheads on existing launchers, or the procurement of new nuclear bombers." [7] Subsequent events have made it abundantly clear that every one of these openings will be exploited to the absolute maximum—more so, perhaps, than if the treaty had not been signed in the first place. The "success" of having achieved even a limited treaty agreement creates an aura of good feeling in which the behavior of those responsible for it is examined less critically than otherwise. It is hard to resist concluding from all this that arms limitation talks are not likely to accomplish anything very significant.

It might be possible to break this deadlock if we actually *wish* to do so (a debatable assumption)—by adopting a policy of graduated unilateral *initiatives*. Such a policy was advocated some years ago by Charles Osgood. The arms race, Osgood observes,

> is a case of graduated, but reciprocal, unilateral action. It is obviously unilateral, in that the nation developing a new weapon, increasing its stockpile, or setting up a new military base, does not make its action contingent upon any agreement with the other side. It is reciprocal because each increment in military power by one side provides the stimulus for intensified efforts by the other side to catch up and get ahead. [8]

Thus, Osgood believes, "the arms race provides a model for its own reversal." [9] Graduated, reciprocal, unilateral action can move in either direction; the spiral need not always be upward.

Osgood provides a number of criteria for appropriate unilateral initiatives toward nuclear disarmament. They are stated as follows: [10]

Our unilateral acts must be perceived by an opponent as reducing his external threat.

Our unilateral acts must be accompanied by explicit invitations to reciprocation.

Unilateral acts must be executed regardless of prior commitment by the opponent to reciprocate.

Unilateral acts must be planned in sequences and continued over considerable periods regardless of reciprocation by an opponent.

Unilateral acts must be announced in advance of execution and widely publicized to ally, neutral, and enemy countries as part of a consistent policy.

Unilateral acts must be graduated in risk potential, should they not be reciprocated or should they be exploited by an opponent.

Unilateral acts must be diverse in nature and unpredictable (by an opponent) as to locus of application and timing in series.

Unilateral acts must never endanger our "heartland" or reduce our fundamental capacity for retaliatory second strike.[11]

Unilateral acts of tension-reducing nature must be accompanied by explicit firmness in all areas.

Since the subject of this work is ethics and not strategy or policy, I do not intend to pursue this matter in any further detail. To do so would be merely to duplicate the work that Osgood has already done. My essential purpose in introducing it is to substantiate my conviction that nuclear disarmament is *not* a hopeless dream, despite the difficulties imposed by existing international conditions. Nuclear disarmament is possible. I believe that what we lack is not the means but the will.

I suspect that for this, there are two reasons. (1) Substantial segments of the American economy, and presumably the economies of all major nations, have developed an extremely high stake in the perpetual continuance of arms and of arms-related technologies.[12] (2) An ideology or system of assumptions, long enough maintained, gathers an authority that is very difficult to shake. It comes to be seen as "obvious" or "self-evident" or "beyond question." It is "taken for granted." This status has now been achieved by the apparent truism that a perpetual nuclear arms race, even unto the nth generation (unless war comes first) is the only realistic possibility. Three decades of steadily escalating violence, together with continuing international hostility and suspicion, not to mention the incessant propaganda of the apologists for an exclusively military definition of reality, have generated a climate in which any form of disarmament is looked upon as naïve and utopian. Those who raise the question are tolerated at best as cranks or harmless visionaries; at worst, they are dismissed as dupes of "the enemy." We have allowed ourselves to become locked into a definition of international reality from which any alternatives other than continuing nuclear terror have automatically been excluded as serious options. We need to break this pattern by demonstrating that other alternatives are possible. Perhaps the time has come for another look at the doctrine of graduated unilateral initiatives toward nuclear disarmanent.

A program of unilateral initiatives might well commence with the cancellation, for example, of all ABM systems, MIRVs, the Trident nuclear submarine, the B-1 bomber, and the CVN-70 nuclear aircraft carrier. Most of these have been criticized as militarily needless and financially wasteful.[13] Add to this a drastic reduction of the total nuclear stockpile, which in the United States alone presently includes enough warheads to destroy every living creature and every stick of property in the Soviet Union twenty times over.[14] Such "over-kill" bears no relationship at all to "national security," save in a negative sense! The more destructive power we accrue, the more fragile and dangerous our present existence becomes. The time to reverse the spiral is *now*.

The essential problem of the nuclear age derives from our seizure of the ultimate powers of nature. These powers, in a sense, now belong to us. However terrible the burden of possessing them, we cannot give them back. We have no choice but to take and use them; the ultimate question is, For what ends? This question is not technical; it is ethical and religious. Our answer to it will reflect the kind of men we are, and the nature of our ultimate priorities. So far, the answer has not been very encouraging.

The world has altered radically since 1945. The splitting of the atom brought into being a new reality—a reality that renders obsolete many assumptions of a former age, and makes potentially demonic many of the loyalties of the past. The patriotism of national states, together with the attendant notion of unilateral national "defense," can no longer represent with impunity the ultimate loyalties and procedures of men. In the past such idolatry was merely sinful; today it is potentially fatal. The goal of man must now be a new kind of patriotism—a patriotism that transcends national boundaries to embrace the world. The unit of survival is no longer the nation—it is the human race. This must be the object of our ultimate loyalty. Anything less is viciously irresponsible. "The brotherhood of man," as C. Wright Mills observed, "is now less a goal than an obvious condition of biological survival. Before the world is made safe for American capitalism or Soviet communism or anything else, it had better be made safe for human life." [15]

The road ahead will be difficult and fraught with peril. Peril we cannot avoid, for *all* roads in the modern world are perilous. The crucial difference between them is not how smooth or how rough they are, but where they lead.

# APPENDIX
## CRITERIA: MORALLY JUSTIFIABLE FORCE

AN ETHIC, LIKE THAT OF CHRISTIANITY, BASED ON CONCEP-
tions of love and justice, is essentially pacifistic: to value
the integrity and personhood of our neighbor requires, at
the very least, that we refrain from injuring him. Yet the
demands of love and justice are paradoxical, reflecting the
paradoxical nature of life itself. For the obligations imposed are twofold: (1) to refrain from violence, and (2)
to protect the innocent from harm. Alas, there are many
situations in which these two obligations come into conflict.
The same ethic which demands of me that I treat all men
with respect and refrain from doing violence to them also
lays upon me the obligation to defend them, by violence
if necessary, from the violence of others. The demand that
places me under obligation to protect the innocent from
violence also obliges me by that very fact to use violence,
if need be, against an aggressor.

> While Jesus taught that a disciple in his own case should
> turn the other cheek, he did not enjoin that his disciples
> should lift up the face of another oppressed man for *him*
> to be struck on *his* other cheek.[1]

The moral paradox defined here has traditionally been re-
solved by appeal to a dual principle: (1) that resort to

violence, under certain special conditions, may be justified or even obligatory, and (2) that since violence is at best a necessary *evil*, its occasion and conduct must be hedged about with the most careful and rigid limitations. This principle has long provided a framework for serious ethical reflection upon the justifiable uses of armed force.[2]

Since violence, by its very nature, involves some level of destruction, suffering, or death, the moral presumption is *always* against it. Violence can *never* be self-justifying; those who advocate its use must undertake the burden of proof—demonstrating why, in any given situation, one of the most basic of all principles should be abrogated. Moreover, once resorted to, violence must be very carefully controlled—especially because of its tendency to *escape* control. That which is evil even at best, becomes doubly evil if not subjected to severe restraint. Thus, the intent of all serious ethical reflection on the justifiable uses of armed force is: (1) to delimit the occasions in which force may be justifiably undertaken, and (2) to repudiate the notion that "anything goes" once force has been resorted to.

Thus the fundamental norm governing the use of armed force is that of limitation: justifiable force is, at the very least, *limited* force. Its objectives and conduct must be clearly circumscribed. Even a war of national survival, undertaken against the most vicious aggressor, must be a limited war. Its objectives must be limited: to repel the aggression (not to destroy the enemy nation). Its conduct must be limited: to destroy military targets (not to punish civilian populations). In war, justice means limitation.

The principle of limitation involves two criteria: *discrimination* and *proportionality:*

1. Discrimination means that warfare may under no circumstances be totalized. Since its only valid objective is

the defense of justice and the restoration of peace, its target must be solely the war-making capacity of the opponent, not the general populace and not the total society as such. Thus it discriminates in the selection of targets: its targets are specifically the military forces of the enemy, justifiably to be attacked only because they stand objectively as the bearers of hostile force which cannot be repelled except by an exertion of military counterforce. This being the case, any move to strike at the general populace or the total society, or otherwise to enlarge the target beyond the specific war-making forces of the enemy, is an example of indiscriminate warfare, and may properly be classed as murder. Indiscriminate warfare has become routine in the twentieth century, represented, for example, by the saturation bombing of civilian populations—a practice introduced by fascists but now accepted as licit by all nations.[3]

2. Proportionality means that acts of war which entail destruction, suffering, and death disproportionate with the military objectives being sought are not morally justifiable. If the evil by-products of an act seriously outweigh its desirable primary effects, the act is not permissible. This is a way of saying that in judging the morality of an act, *all* its consequences must be taken into account—not merely those which happen to be of interest to the generals. In the present context the point at issue is the magnitude of destruction, suffering, and death which can be accepted as morally tolerable by-products of military actions whose primary intended consequence is the suppression of unjust force. There is probably no sure means of weighing all the variables against each other; yet it is not difficult to recognize, in principle, that some acts, in their consequences, may be more evil than good, or that some acts may entail

evil by-products so great as to nullify the intended primary consequences. An example of such disproportion carried to its final extremity is expressed by the epitaph to the Vietnamese town of Ban Tre: "We destroyed it in order to save it." There is some question, by now, whether any *other* kind of "salvation" is possible, given the kind of weapons that modern wars are fought with—including "conventional" wars. Thus the possibility suggests itself that, in the "age of Omnipotence," the institution of war itself may be obsolete.

# NOTES

## Chapter 1
### POWER UNLIMITED: A NEW PROBLEM FOR A NEW TIME

1. Harrison Brown and James Real, "Community of Fear," in Walter Millis *et al.*, *A World Without War*, p. 6.

2. *Ibid.*, p. 13.

3. *Ibid.*, p. 6.

4. Jerome D. Frank, *Sanity and Survival: Psychological Aspects of War and Peace*, p. 17. Data from T. Stonier, *Nuclear Disaster* (The World Publishing Company, Meridian Books, 1964).

5. Bert Cochran, *The War System*, p. 26.

6. See the work of Robert Jay Lifton, M.D.

7. The term "omnipotence" in this context is not, of course, used as an absolute. *Relative to human life*, "omnipotent" power is the power to cancel out all other human powers—which means, finally, the power to cancel out human existence itself. Such "omnipotence" is nothing, if not ironic.

8. Perhaps the closest analogy to this state of mind is the inability of each man, in more than an academic way, to believe in the reality of his own eventual demise. We "know" (intellectually) of the fate that lies in store, but we do not truly "believe" (existentially) in its reality. Of course this sense of "psychic unreality" is a necessary "screening device" to protect us against an awareness that would otherwise be unbearable. But it is, I think, more than that. The state of our own

nonbeing is so vastly discontinuous with everything we now know that we cannot make the radical "shift" required to imagine it. Even to imagine ourselves as not being requires the positing of ourselves as some form of "presence" to do the imagining.

## Chapter 2
### REFLECTIONS FOR AN AGE OF OMNIPOTENCE

1. Brigid Brophy, *Black Ship to Hell*, p. 351.

2. The personalistic terminology here should not necessarily be taken to suggest the popular image of a "divine being" who "exists" in some sense independently from the rest of reality, and for his own reasons commands certain things and prohibits others. To speak of "God" is to speak, as best we can, of *reality in its ultimate character*, of what finally determines, supports, and commands our lives. To speak of God's "will" is to acknowledge that reality in its ultimate character makes "demands" on us that we cannot ignore without disastrous results. Theologically, to acknowledge God's "will" is to acknowledge that the order of values is not arbitrary, or strictly "invented," but contains an element of "objectivity" which stands over against us as commanding. "Right" and "wrong" really are right and wrong; and though our understanding of right and wrong is always imperfect, and at times grossly distorted, our experiences of right and wrong do reflect, however obscurely, something objectively present in the nature of things. (This affirmation lies within the realm of faith, and cannot be "proved." Nonetheless, it is not without supporting evidence.)

3. This is true in the short run; it is not always true in the long run. Every major human decision, especially when magnified by technology, carries consequences that elude prediction and control by those who initiate it.

4. George Bernard Shaw, *Man and Superman*, Act III.

5. William James, *The Moral Equivalent of War*, p. 2. This essay was originally delivered before an assembly of American peace societies in 1905.

6. "Men's best talents and energies have been devoted to

perfecting means of destroying each other, and societies continue to spend more of their economic and human resources on preparing for and waging war than on any other enterprise. Civilizations rise and fall, but the development of arms technology has never faltered." Frank, *op. cit.*, p. 41.

7. Lewis Mumford, *Technics and Civilization,* p. 87.

8. *Ibid.,* p. 88.

9. *Ibid.*

10. *Ibid.,* p. 90.

11. *Ibid.,* p. 91.

12. The only way to "control" such a weapon in the long run, as this book will seek to make clear, is to get rid of it.

## Chapter 3
### DETERRENCE: THE DEADLY PARADOX

1. Frank, *op. cit.*, p. 139.

2. It ought to be noted that the instability inherent in nuclear deterrence as such is in danger of being increased by the deployment of MIRVs (Multiple Independently Targetable Reentry Vehicles). Since it is, of course, much easier to knock out a single warhead than it is to knock out five or six, there is pressure, in the event of crisis, to destroy MIRVs while they are still on the launch pad and their multiple warheads are still contained in a single package. Thus the deployment of MIRVs is a provocative act, which increases the advantage of a first strike by the adversary.

3. John C. Bennett, *Foreign Policy in Christian Perspective,* p. 113.

4. This is perceived, for example, even by Herman Kahn, who on one occasion wrote: "Aside from the ideological differences and the problem of security itself, there does not seem to be any objective quarrel between the United States and Russia that justifies the risks and costs that we subject each other to." Stanford Research Institute *Journal,* 1959, cited by Robert F. Drinan, S.J., *Vietnam and Armageddon: Peace, War and the Christian Conscience,* p. 159.

5. Bennett, *op. cit.,* p. 113.

6. Most strategists believe that for such an expressed will-

ingness to be fully credible it must be actual: a stated willingness that was not actual would be eventually detected, through security leaks, etc. See, for instance, Herman Kahn, *On Thermonuclear War*, p. 185.

7. James W. Douglass, *The Non-Violent Cross: A Theology of Revolution and Peace*, p. 161.

## Chapter 4
### ESCALATING THE ACCEPTABLE

1. Robert C. Batchelder, *The Irreversible Decision: 1939–1950*, p. 174.

2. *Ibid.*, p. 175.

3. See Raphael Littauer and Norman Uphoff (eds.), *The Air War in Indochina*, rev. ed., pp. 39–40.

4. Testimony of Jon Floyd before the Winter Soldier Investigation, Detroit, Jan. 31 to Feb. 1–2, 1971. Quoted in *American Report*, Jan. 28, 1972.

5. See Noam Chomsky, *At War with Asia*, p. 98.

6. This process may be clearly seen in the changed public attitudes toward military conscription. Once regarded as a practice, because of its repugnance to democratic principles, only to be employed in time of national emergency, conscription is now almost universally accepted in American society as a permanent and legitimate institution. We have lived with it for so long now that any other social arrangement seems inconceivable.

7. Batchelder, *op. cit.*, p. 172.

8. Quoted in Batchelder, *op. cit.*, p. 172, and in Roland H. Bainton, *Christian Attitudes Toward War and Peace: A Historical Survey and Critical Re-evaluation*, p. 228.

9. Quoted in Batchelder, *op. cit.*, p. 173.

10. Quoted in Bainton, *op. cit.*, p. 225.

11. *Ibid.*

12. David Irving, *The Destruction of Dresden*, p. 48.

13. *Ibid.*, p. 62.

14. *Ibid.*, p. 209, *passim*.

15. Batchelder, *op. cit.*, p. 182.

16. Quoted by Batchelder, *op. cit.*, pp. 180–181.

17. *The Christian Conscience and Weapons of Mass Destruction* (The Dun Commission), Report of a Special Commission Appointed by the Federal Council of Churches of Christ in America, Department of International Justice and Goodwill, December 1950, p. 23.

18. Batchelder, *op. cit.*, p. 181.

19. John C. Ford, S.J., "The Morality of Obliteration Bombing," *Theological Studies*, Vol. V, No. 3 (Sept. 1944), pp. 302, 303, 304.

20. Batchelder, *op. cit.*, pp. 186–187.

21. John Courtney Murray, S.J., "Theology and Modern War," in *Morality and Modern Warfare: The State of the Question*, ed. by William J. Nagle, p. 88.

22. The United States has toyed with the notion of "counterforce" nuclear war since 1962. The idea was first publicly introduced by Secretary of Defense Robert McNamara in a speech in June of that year at the University of Michigan. In the course of that speech, McNamara said: "The United States has come to the conclusion that, to the extent feasible, basic military strategy in a possible general nuclear war should be approached in much the same way that more conventional military operations have been regarded in the past. That is to say, principal military objectives, in the event of a nuclear war stemming from a major attack on the [NATO] Alliance, should be the destruction of the enemy's military forces, not of his civilian population." One source of this quotation is Paul Ramsey, "The Limits of Nuclear War," in his book *The Just War: Force and Political Responsibility*, pp. 211–212.

23. See, for example, Cochran, *op. cit.*, pp. 93–94: "It is impossible in industrial societies to separate nuclear forces from populations. Military sites are close to cities, and when weapons are as destructive as nuclear warheads are, even were they to score bull's-eyes on targets, they would vaporize the surrounding areas for miles around and contaminate entire countries and continents."

24. The effects of a nuclear blast are not confined only to the time of attack. Survivors of even such "small" bombs as

those which destroyed Hiroshima and Nagasaki are, a quarter century later, *still dying* from malignancies connected with atomic radiation.

25. See John C. Ford, S.J., "The Hydrogen Bombing of Cities," in Nagle (ed.), *Morality and Modern Warfare,* pp. 98–103.

26. According to Dean Acheson, "Our allies would see at once that the proposed strategy would consign them to a fate more devastating than would compliance with the demands of the Soviet Union. The merit of this strategy, they would be told, would lie in its avoidance of 'all-out' nuclear war, but it would seem to be all-out enough for them." Cited in Cochran, *op. cit.,* pp. 70–71.

27. The amount of devastation made possible with modern "conventional" weapons is perhaps best typified by the B-52, originally designed for delivery of nuclear weapons. Its replacement by missile systems led to its adaptation as an instrument of "conventional" bombing. Yet the notion of what is "conventional" has escalated rather sharply in recent years under the impact of more advanced technologies. The B-52, according to Orville Schell, is "one of the most indiscriminate and destructive weapons in the history of warfare" (*The Boston Globe,* May 31, 1971). The typical B-52 strike is made by six planes, each carrying thirty tons of bombs, which they unload in a fraction of a minute from seven miles up, leaving a swath of practically total destruction half a mile wide and three miles long (Orville Schell, in *American Report,* April 21, 1972). In describing their effects, Schell wrote: "The B-52 'carpet-bombing raids' left mile after mile of shattered jungle, smallpox-like craters, and scars in the yellow earth. Their paths of destruction stretched over mountain tops, across rivers, and into valleys, like some chaotic attempt to build a super-highway from the air." (*Ibid.*) According to Littauer and Uphoff, "To witness such a raid is to witness a disaster of major proportions" (*The Air War in Indochina,* p. 56).

Between B-52 "carpet-bombing," napalm, herbicides, and the Rome Plow, the United States managed in seven years' time to alter the very shape of the land. One description notes: "Bomb craters beyond counting, the dead gray and black fields, forests that have been defoliated and scorched by napalm, land that has been plowed flat to destroy Vietcong hiding places. And everywhere can be seen the piles of ashes forming the outlines of huts and houses, to show where hamlets once stood." (Tom Buckley, *New York Times Magazine*, Nov. 23, 1969.) With such results as this, who needs nuclear weapons?

28. "Nuclear War Games," *Hard Times*, May 25 to June 1, 1970.

29. *Ibid.*

30. Thomas E. Murray, *Nuclear Policy for War and Peace*, p. 65.

31. Detailed documentations of these and similar policies can be found in many current works; for example: Littauer and Uphoff, *op. cit.*; Barry Weisberg (ed.), *Ecocide in Indochina: The Ecology of War*; Richard A. Falk, Gabriel Kolko, and Robert Jay Lifton (eds.), *Crimes of War*; Chomsky, *op. cit.*; Frank Harvey, *Air War—Vietnam*.

32. Thomas Murray, *Nuclear Policy for War and Peace*, pp. 49–50.

33. *Ibid.*, p. 50.

34. For a description of the way this process currently operates in the U.S. military, see Richard J. Barnet, *The Economy of Death*, pp. 48 ff.

35. Thomas Murray, *Nuclear Policy for War and Peace*, p. 50.

36. *Ibid.*, p. 33.

37. *Ibid.*, p. 40. See also John K. Moriarty, "Technology, Strategy, and Military Policy," in Nagle (ed.), *Morality and Modern Warfare*, p. 38; and Cochran, *op. cit.*, pp. 66–67.

38. The Billy Mitchell case is the most famous example of this. It should also be noted that the British High Command during World War I opposed use of the machine gun, the tank, and the convoy system, until Lloyd George overrode their objections. See Cochran, *op. cit.*, pp. 63–64.

39. From Remarks Before United Press International Editors and Publishers, San Francisco, California, Monday, Sept. 18, 1967. A complete transcript of this address may be found in Ralph E. Lapp, *The Weapons Culture*, pp. 204–220. This quotation, p. 218.

40. Paul Ramsey, "The Limits of Nuclear War," *The Just War,* p. 213.

41. Paul Ramsey, *War and the Christian Conscience: How Shall Modern War Be Conducted Justly?* p. 163.

42. The term "double effect" refers to the foreknown but unintended death of noncombatants as an unavoidable concomitant of military action. According to Ramsey: "Acts of war which directly intend and directly effect the death of noncombatants are to be classed morally with murder, and are never excusable. . . . A desired and desirable victory may, however, justify conduct in warfare that causes the deaths, and is foreknown to cause the deaths, of non-combatants indirectly" —that is, as a by-product of military action directed at legitimate targets. According to Catholic moralist Gordon Zahn, "double effect," in the context of nuclear strategy discussion, "is fast becoming a moral slide rule by which almost any act of war can be justified."

43. Paul Ramsey, "The Case for Making Just War Possible," *The Just War,* p. 153. Italics mine.

44. And there is no reason to suppose, I should think, that initiating the one would necessarily forestall the other. Quite the contrary: "small" wars are likely to lead to "big" wars, especially when even the "small" wars are pretty big to start with. Wars of *any* kind tend to get out of hand, and nuclear wars—large or small—would, it seems reasonable to suppose, display this regrettable tendency rather more than most.

45. The Indochina war is the most glaring current example of this. Never before in human history have a people been so ferociously, savagely, and systematically punished—all in the name of objectives which even the staunchest proponents of the war now admit have only marginal connection with the national interest. The prevailing moral climate is of such a nature as to lend sanction to virtually unlimited violence, as long as (1) the machinery is available to perpetrate it, and (2) even the most marginal objectives can be adduced to justify it.

## Chapter 5
### HORROR DOMESTICATED: THE SEMANTICS OF MEGADEATH

1. For example, Ernst Cassirer, Suzanne Langer, S. I. Hayakawa, H. N. Wieman.

2. Henry Nelson Wieman, *Religious Inquiry*, p. 142.

3. *Ibid.*, p. 144.

4. George Orwell, "Politics and the English Language," in his *Collected Essays*, p. 363.

5. Justus George Lawler, *Nuclear War: The Ethic, The Rhetoric, The Reality*, p. 96.

6. *Ibid.*, p. 97.

7. Philip Slater, *The Pursuit of Loneliness: American Culture at the Breaking Point*, p. 38.

8. Herman Kahn, "Some Comments on Controlled War," in *The Debate Over Thermonuclear Strategy*, Problems in American Civilization, ed. by Arthur I. Waskow. Originally published in *Limited Strategic War*, ed. by Klaus Knorr and Thornton Read (Frederick A. Praeger, Inc., 1962). This citation, p. 21.

9. Lawler, *op. cit.*, p. 96.


## Chapter 6
### ANTISEPTIC WAR:
### THE PROBLEM OF PERSONAL RESPONSIBILITY

1. Ralph E. Lapp, *Kill and Overkill: The Strategy of Annihilation*, p. 22.

2. Günther Anders, "Reflections on the H Bomb," in *Man Alone: Alienation in Modern Society*, ed. by Eric and Mary Josephson, pp. 292–293.

3. Anatol Rapoport, *Strategy and Conscience*, pp. 243–244.

4. Philip Berrigan, S.S.J., from an untitled, mimeographed sermon delivered at Boston University, Oct. 1, 1965.

5. Rapoport, *op. cit.*, p. 285.

6. The thesis that the sense of personal responsibility bears an inverse relationship to the perceived "distance" be-

tween the self and others has received important empirical validation by the well-known experiment in which Stanley Milgram tested the willingness of subjects, under various conditions, to obey commands supposedly involving the infliction of pain upon other persons. Each subject was told to administer electric shocks of increasing strength—from "slight" (30 volts) to "severe" (450 volts)—to "victims" in four different relationships to the subject himself: (1) in a different room, and neither seen nor heard; (2) in a different room, but audible over a loudspeaker; (3) in the same room; and (4) in physical contact with the subject (the subject had to administer the shock directly). Among the results of this experiment was the indication of a markedly greater willingness on the part of subjects to administer "severe shocks" as the distance between subject and "victim" increased, from a low percentage in (4) to a very high percentage in (1). Apparently moral inhibitions against violence tend to be seriously attenuated when the pain and suffering it causes are remote and therefore experienced as less "real." See Stanley Milgram, "Some Conditions of Obedience and Disobedience to Authority," *Human Relations*, Feb. 1965, pp. 57–75.

7. According to the authors of *The Air War in Indochina*, a retired general who had studied at the National War College reported having sensed a pattern in the way in which student officers there responded in the context of war game scenarios. "When faced with situations requiring either a diplomatic or a military response to a given crisis, experienced Navy PT-boat commanders tended to favor diplomatic solutions, while Polaris submarine commanders preferred tactical or strategic military responses. Similar distinctions were observed between Army infantry and artillery commanders, and between Air Force Tactical Air Command and Strategic Air Command officers. He concluded that those officers who were confronted directly with the consequences of their actions in the form of human lives lost, whether adversary, neutral, or allied, were more reluctant to resort to military solutions. Those officers whose weapons systems delivered death remotely were much more willing to call awesome amounts of fire-power into play." Littauer and Uphoff (eds.), *The Air War in Indochina*, p. 159.

8. *Ibid.*, p. 159. This observation is made with reference to American air warfare in Indochina. It applies equally, of course, to *any* form of automated, remote-control warfare.

9. *Ibid.*, p. 164.

10. *Ibid.*

11. George L. Weiss, "The Air Force's Secret Electronic War," *Military Aircraft*, 1971. Detailed descriptions and analyses of the "electronic battlefield" may be found in Littauer and Uphoff (eds.), *The Air War in Indochina* and in *Investigation Into Electronic Battlefield Program*, Hearings Before the Electronic Battlefield Subcommittee of the Committee on Armed Services, United States Senate, Ninety-first Congress, Second Session, Nov. 1970.

12. "Subjectivity" may refer simply to the misinterpretation of data; or it *could* have a deeper significance. Machines, as one commentator has observed, "do not bleed, die, frag their officers, become addicts, protest, or write revealing letters home." Orville Schell, "Electronic Death," *Christianity and Crisis*, Vol. XXXII, No. 8 (May 15, 1972), p. 121.

13. "A seismic detector cannot tell the difference between a truck full of arms and a school bus; a urine sniffer cannot tell a military shelter from a woodcutter's shack." Littauer and Uphoff (eds.), *The Air War in Indochina*, p. 158.

14. *Ibid.*, p. 159.

15. *Ibid.*, Ch. 12.

16. It may be that the doing of warfare this way has political objectives too. A distant war waged primarily by machines is, from the point of view of the American citizenry, a "low profile" war: while horrendously destructive to the "enemy," its cost in American lives is minuscule. A war of this type could go on for years, inflicting untold agonies upon foreign populations, yet impinge so marginally upon the public consciousness of America as to cause hardly a ripple of protest. Thus, the triumph of modern technology has been to realize the prediction of George Orwell's *1984*: that "war involves very small numbers of people, mostly highly trained specialists. The fighting . . . takes place on the vague frontiers whose whereabouts the average man can only guess at."

17. Gen. William Westmoreland, Address to Association

of the United States Army, Sheraton Park Hotel, Washington, D.C., Oct. 14, 1969.

18. Quoted in *American Report,* Oct. 22, 1971.

19. Bainton, *op. cit.,* p. 223.

20. Anders, *loc. cit.,* p. 294.

21. Konrad Lorenz, *On Aggression,* tr. by Marjorie Kerr Wilson, pp. 242–243.

22. John C. Bennett, "Moral Urgencies in the Nuclear Context," in *Nuclear Weapons and the Conflict of Conscience,* ed. by John C. Bennett, p. 102. Italics mine.

23. Anders, *loc. cit.,* p. 295.

24. *Ibid.,* p. 294.

25. *Ibid.,* p. 295.

26. *Ibid.,* p. 296.

27. *Ibid.,* p. 297.

28. *Ibid.,* p. 294.

## Chapter 7
### THE ANTHROPOLOGY OF TECHNICIZED "AGGRESSION"

1. Anthropologist Ralph Holloway defines "instinct" as "a quite specific response pattern, invariant in its development, maturation, and expression, which occurs in the presence of a quite specific cluster of stimuli from the environment. As such, it is regarded as an innate, genetically determined pattern, which comes about without reference to, or in the absence of learning." Ralph Holloway, "Human Aggression: The Need for a Species-Specific Framework," in *War: The Anthropology of Armed Conflict and Aggression,* ed. by Morton Fried *et al.,* p. 33.

2. "Human aggression and human territoriality are products of social systems, not of biological systems, and they must be treated as such." Kenneth E. Boulding, "Am I a Man or a Mouse—or Both?" in *Man and Aggression,* ed. by M. F. Ashley Montagu, p. 88.

3. "The notable thing about *human* behavior is that it is learned. Everything a human being does as such he has had to learn from other human beings. From any dominance of biologically or inherited predetermined reactions that may prevail

in the behavior of other animals, man has moved into a zone of adaptation in which his behavior is dominated by learned responses. It is within the dimension of culture, the learned, that man grows, develops, and has his being as a behaving organism." Montagu (ed.), *Man and Aggression,* p. xii.

4. L. Berkowitz, "The Concept of Aggression Drive: Some Additional Considerations," in *Advances in Experimental Social Psychology,* Vol. II, ed. by L. Berkowitz (Academic Press, Inc., 1965), p. 302. Quoted by Ralph Holloway, *loc. cit.,* p. 32.

5. Recent researches have called public attention to the possibility of developing an "anti-aggression" pill, designed to lower the aggression levels in people generally, thereby presumably fostering more amicable human relations and reducing the incidence of crime, violence, and war. I do not share these benign hopes. Such a device would raise serious problems. Its potential for mischief is truly alarming. The crucial issue, of course, is: Who would *administer* the pills, and who would (be compelled to) *take* them? See Aldous Huxley, *Brave New World.*

6. Lorenz, *op. cit.,* p. 129.

7. *Ibid.,* p. 240.

8. Anthony Storr, *Human Aggression,* p. 112.

9. Lorenz, *op. cit.,* p. 241.

10. Frank, *op. cit.,* p. 51.

11. See, for example, Littauer and Uphoff (eds.), *The Air War in Indochina,* p. 126): "[T]he technology of air war evolves very rapidly, leaving behind any detailed regulations. . . . Even broad-based principles may be difficult if not impossible to apply when the weapons systems in use are undreamed of by those who earlier formulated the fundamental principles." This observation is not limited, of course, to the conduct of air warfare; air warfare merely happens to be that form of warfare in which technological advance is most rapid.

12. John Poppy, "Violence: We Can End It," *Look,* Vol. XXXIII, No. 12 (June 10, 1969), p. 22.

13. Richard B. Gregg, *The Power of Nonviolence,* second rev. ed. pp. 54–55.

14. I am indebted to Herbert Marcuse for the genesis of this idea. See his "Aggressiveness in Advanced Industrial So-

ciety," in his book *Negations: Essays in Critical Theory,* pp. 263–264. On the other hand, Marcuse seems to believe that *all* technologized aggression displays the characteristics here described as "delegated." In this respect, I believe him to be grossly mistaken.

15. A man with a weapon may in fact be led to commit considerable amounts of destruction on the strength of impulsiveness alone—for fun, as it were—simply because the act of killing, especially at great distances, is so easy to perform. There is surely little if any "aggression" involved in the random shooting at undefended villages in Vietnam by gunboats in the Mekong River and by helicopter gunships: "They seemed to fire whimsically and in passing even though they were not being shot at from the ground nor could they identify the people as NLF. They did it impulsively for fun, using the farmers for targets as if in a hunting mood. They are hunting Asians." From a news article by Hatsuichi Honda in *Asahi Shimbun* in the fall of 1967. Cited by Chomsky, *op. cit.,* p. 99.

## Chapter 8
### UNINTENDED WAR: THE PRESUMPTION OF PERFECT CONTROL

1. Arthur I. Waskow, *The Limits of Defense,* p. 41.

2. Thomas E. Murray, *op. cit.,* p. 46.

3. Thomas E. Murray, "Morality and Security—The Forgotten Equation," *America,* Vol. XCVI, No. 9 (Dec. 1, 1956), p. 260.

4. See especially Chapter 4, above, for the discussion of the way in which moral perception can be altered, without our "consent," by factors that are unrecognized or unadmitted as having any impact on our decisions.

5. Lapp, *Kill and Overkill,* p. 86.

6. There has never been a war—even the most "justified" —that did not involve at least *some* degree of wanton, criminal activity on *both* sides. Indeed, the sense of having a "just cause" to fight for is *itself* one of the factors responsible for the erosion of restraints in the conduct of violence. The more righteous the cause, the more latitude seems to be permitted in its behalf. Much has been written during recent years concern-

ing distinctions between the "just war" and the "crusade." See, e.g., Roland Bainton, *Christian Attitudes Toward War and Peace*. The trouble, as Bainton suggests, is that every war is seen by its participants as a "just" war, and every "just" war tends to become a "crusade."

7. John R. Raser, "The Failure of Failsafe," *Trans-action*, Vol. VI, No. 3 (Jan. 1969), p. 18.

8. Seymour Melman, *The Peace Race*, pp. 10–11.

9. Frank, *op. cit.*, p. 55.

10. Lloyd V. Berkner, from an article in *Foreign Affairs*, 1958; cited by Lapp, *Kill and Overkill*. Further bibliographical data not supplied.

11. See, for example, Erwin Knoll, "More Weapons for the 'Generation of Peace,'" *The Progressive*, Aug. 1972, p. 16; and Friends Committee on National Legislation, *Washington Newsletter*, No. 349 (June 1973), p. 3.

12. Frank, *op. cit.*, p. 57.

13. Roy Grinker and John Spiegel, reporting on studies of aircraft combat crews during World War II. Quoted by Raser, "The Failure of Failsafe," *loc. cit.*, p. 16. Further bibliographical data not supplied.

14. John V. Phelps *et al.*, *Accidental War: Some Dangers in the 1960's*, Mershon National Security Program, Ohio State University (June 28, 1960). Quoted in Melman, *op. cit.*

15. *Air Force Manual 160-55*, "Guidance for Implementing Human Reliability Program," Feb. 28, 1962. Quoted by Frank, *op. cit.*, p. 57.

16. In "The Failure of Failsafe," John Raser reported on three experiments in which men were tested for their responses to stress. In the first two, military officers were involved in the role of decision makers in "games" of international affairs, in which at various stages they were confronted with crisis situations threatening the achievement of their objectives. As the crises intensified, "the men lost some of their ability to evaluate information, were able to consider fewer alternative courses of action, and tended to be less flexible. In short, as threat increased and time for response decreased, their ability to cope with the situation was lessened."

The third experiment subjected to computer analysis the

behavior of European decision makers during the six-week crisis period preceding the outbreak of World War I. The results were the same. As the crisis intensified, "the decision-makers saw fewer alternatives, they distorted their position in relation to others, their messages became more stereotyped, and they began to lose the ability to think in long-range terms, focusing their attention instead on extricating themselves from the current problem—and damn the long-range consequences. Thus, as threat intensified, their ability to think and act rationally degenerated."

17. Melman, *op. cit.*, p. 14.

18. Raser, *loc. cit.*, p. 18.

19. Herman Kahn, *On Thermonuclear War*, Lect. III, Ch. x, pp. 514–515.

20. J. William Fulbright, *The Arrogance of Power*, p. 160.

## Chapter 9
### GETTING THE GENIE BACK IN THE BOTTLE

1. After seeing what the exercise of American "responsibility" (read: military power) has done to the land and people of Indochina, to name only the most nakedly obvious example, one is tempted to conclude that a world entirely dominated by American power is not a very engaging prospect either.

2. The "better dead than Red" game can be played much more safely, of course, when the power relations are asymmetrical: that is, when a very large and powerful nation decides to engage a very small, weak nation. In that instance, the name of the game is more aptly expressed as: "Better *you* should be dead than Red." Such a game is easy to play, since of course there is no danger of retaliation, as long as the more powerful allies of the small, weak nation are treated with appropriate solicitude.

3. Herbert Butterfield, *International Conflict in the Twentieth Century—A Christian View*, p. 95.

4. Bennett, *Foreign Policy in Christian Perspective*, p. 105.

5. *Ibid.*, p. 112.

6. Edgar M. Bottome, *The Balance of Terror: A Guide to the Arms Race*, p. 148.

7. Erwin Knoll, *loc. cit.*, p. 16.

8. Charles Osgood, "Reciprocal Initiative," *The Liberal Papers*, ed. by James Roosevelt (Doubleday & Company, Inc., 1962). Reprinted in *The Debate Over Thermonuclear Strategy*, ed. by Arthur I. Waskow, pp. 69–81. This passage, p. 71.

9. *Ibid.*

10. Their statement, and accompanying discussion, may be found on pp. 71–75 of the article by Osgood cited above.

11. Osgood believes that "this minimum capacity for effective deterrence should not be reduced by unilateral action (even though other forms of armament could be), but rather its elimination could be arrived at through negotiation, in the atmosphere of greater confidence and trust produced by the policy we are discussing."

12. For detailed analyses of this trend, see, for example, Richard J. Barnet, *The Economy of Death*, and Seymour Melman, *Pentagon Capitalism: The Political Economy of War* (McGraw-Hill Book Co., Inc., 1970).

13. See, for example, Hon. Robert F. Drinan, Remarks in the House of Representatives, *Congressional Record*, Vol. CXIX, No. 34 (March 5, 1973).

14. See page 122. According to estimates made by Richard Barnet, "one hundred nuclear weapons landing on the Soviet Union would for practical purposes destroy the society" (*The Economy of Death*, p. 24). Thus, the actual stockpiles in the United States alone represent an "overkill" capacity of more than 6000 percent!

15. C. Wright Mills, *The Causes of World War Three*, p. 172.


## *Appendix*
### CRITERIA: MORALLY JUSTIFIABLE FORCE

1. Paul Ramsey, "Justice in War," *The Just War*, p. 143.

2. The attempt to elaborate norms governing the justifiable resort to, and the morally proper use of, armed force, has

been a major effort of theologians and philosophers since Augustine (354–430) first set down his own reflections on the "just war" in Book 19 of *The City of God*. These efforts have not, alas, been rewarded by enthusiastic observance on the part of the international community. In this respect, however, they are not very different from ethical prescriptions generally, whose power to influence human conduct has always been limited at best.

3. It is widely suggested these days that now, in the age of "total war," the principle of restraint is "obsolete." Those who, for example, defend the policy of B-52 strategic bombing as currently practiced by American forces in Southeast Asia—one of the most indiscriminate methods of warfare ever devised— have implicit recourse to the notion that absolutely anything is permissible that hurts the enemy or "destroys his will to resist." See, for example, Robert M. Kipp, "Counterinsurgency from 30,000 Feet: The B-52 in Vietnam," *Air University Review*, Vol. XIX, No. 2 (Jan.–Feb. 1968), pp. 13–20. Military thinking of this kind does not appear to recognize any principle of restraint whatever, other than "military necessity." It must be clearly affirmed, in response to this, that moral principles have not become invalid simply because we can now violate them more readily and more grossly than we did in the past. Indeed, just the reverse is the case. The growing readiness to plan, to condone, and to employ total violence merely because it happens to be "militarily effective" demands that the principle of moral restraint be enunciated more clearly and forcefully than ever before. It is the obligation of all men of conscience to "say 'No'"—to declare forthrightly that the concept of unlimited violence, or total war, cannot under any circumstances be condoned.

# BIBLIOGRAPHY

Anders, Günther, "Reflections on the H Bomb," in *Man Alone: Alienation in Modern Society*, ed. by Eric and Mary Josephson. Dell Publishing Company, Inc., 1962.

Ardrey, Robert, *African Genesis: A Personal Investigation Into the Animal Origins and Nature of Man*. Atheneum Publishers, 1961.

———— *The Territorial Imperative: A Personal Inquiry Into the Animal Origins of Property and Nations*. Atheneum Publishers, 1966.

Bainton, Roland H., *Christian Attitudes Toward War and Peace: A Historical Survey and Critical Re-evaluation*. Abingdon Press, 1960.

Barnet, Richard J., *The Economy of Death*. Atheneum Publishers, 1969.

Batchelder, Robert C., *The Irreversible Decision: 1939–1950*. Houghton Mifflin Company, 1962.

Bennett, John C., *Foreign Policy in Christian Perspective*. Charles Scribner's Sons, 1966.

———— (ed.), *Nuclear Weapons and the Conflict of Conscience*. Charles Scribner's Sons, 1962.

Bottome, Edgar M., *The Balance of Terror: A Guide to the Arms Race*. Beacon Press, Inc., 1971.

Branfman, Fred, *Voices from the Plain of Jars: Life Under an Air War*. Harper & Row, Publishers, Inc., 1972.

———— and Cohn, Steve, "A New Kind of Winter Soldier," *American Report*, Oct. 22, 1971, p. 5.

Brophy, Brigid, *Black Ship to Hell.* Harcourt, Brace and World, Inc., 1962.

Butterfield, Herbert, *International Conflict in the Twentieth Century—A Christian View.* Harper & Brothers, 1960.

Chomsky, Noam, *At War with Asia.* Random House, Inc., 1970.

Cochran, Bert, *The War System.* The Macmillan Company, 1965.

Douglass, James W., *The Non-Violent Cross: A Theology of Revolution and Peace.* The Macmillan Company, 1966.

Drinan, Robert F., S.J., Remarks in the House of Representatives, *Congressional Record,* Vol. CXIX, No. 34 (March 5, 1973).

———— *Vietnam and Armageddon: Peace, War and the Christian Conscience.* Sheed & Ward, Inc., 1970.

Falk, Richard A.; Kolko, Gabriel; and Lifton, Robert Jay (eds.), *Crimes of War.* Random House, Inc., 1971.

Fleming, D. F., *Does Deterrence Deter?* A Study and Commentary in the Beyond Deterrence Series. American Friends Service Committee, 1962.

Ford, John C., S.J., "The Morality of Obliteration Bombing," *Theological Studies,* Vol. V, No. 3 (Sept. 1944), pp. 261–309.

Frank, Jerome D., *Sanity and Survival: Psychological Aspects of War and Peace.* Random House, Inc., 1967.

Fried, Morton, *et al.* (eds.), *War: The Anthropology of Armed Conflict and Aggression.* The Natural History Press, 1967.

Friends Committee on National Legislation. *Washington Newsletter,* No. 349 (June, 1973).

Fulbright, J. William, *The Arrogance of Power.* Random House, Inc., 1966.

Gregg, Richard B., *The Power of Nonviolence,* second rev. ed. Schocken Books, Inc., 1966.

Harvey, Frank, *Air War—Vietnam.* Bantam Books, Inc., 1967.

*Impact of the Vietnam War.* Prepared for the use of Committee on Foreign Relations, United States Senate, by the Foreign Affairs Division, Congressional Research Service, June 1971.

*Investigation Into Electronic Battlefield Program.* Hearings before the Electronic Battlefield Subcommittee of the Preparedness Investigating Subcommittee of the Committee on

Armed Services, United States Senate, Ninety-first Congress, Second Session, Nov. 1970.

Irving, David, *The Destruction of Dresden*. Holt, Rinehart & Winston, Inc., 1963.

James, William, *The Moral Equivalent of War*. Fellowship Publications, n.d.

Kahn, Herman, *On Thermonuclear War*. Princeton University Press, 1960.

Kipp, Robert M., "Counterinsurgency from 30,000 Feet: The B-52 in Vietnam," *Air University Review*, Vol. XIX, No. 2 (Jan.–Feb. 1968), pp. 13–20.

Knoll, Erwin, "More Weapons for the 'Generation of Peace,'" *The Progressive*, Vol. XXXVI, No. 8 (Aug. 1972), pp. 14–16.

*Laos: April 1971*. A Staff Report Prepared for the Use of the Subcommittee on U.S. Security Agreements and Commitments Abroad of the Committee on Foreign Relations, United States Senate, Aug. 1971.

Lapp, Ralph E., *Kill and Overkill: The Strategy of Annihilation*. Basic Books, Inc., 1962.

——— *The Weapons Culture*. W. W. Norton & Company, Inc., 1968.

Lawler, Justus George, *Nuclear War: The Ethic, The Rhetoric, The Reality*. The Newman Press, 1965.

Littauer, Raphael, and Uphoff, Norman (eds.), with Air War Study Group, Cornell University, *The Air War in Indochina*, rev. ed. Beacon Press, Inc., 1972.

Lorenz, Konrad, *On Aggression*, tr. by Marjorie Kerr Wilson. Harcourt, Brace and World, Inc., 1966.

Marcuse, Herbert, "Aggressiveness in Advanced Industrial Society," *Negations: Essays in Critical Theory*. Beacon Press, Inc., 1968.

Marrin, Albert (ed.), *War and the Christian Conscience: From Augustine to Martin Luther King, Jr.* Henry Regnery Company, 1971.

Melman, Seymour, *The Peace Race*. George Braziller, Inc., 1962.

Millis, Walter, and Real, James, *The Abolition of War*. The Macmillan Company, 1963.

—————— et al., A World Without War. Washington Square Press, Inc., 1961.

Mills, C. Wright, The Causes of World War Three. Ballantine Books, Inc., 1958.

Montagu, M. F. Ashley (ed.), Man and Aggression. Oxford University Press, 1968.

Mumford, Lewis, The Myth of the Machine: The Pentagon of Power. Harcourt Brace Jovanovich, Inc., 1964, 1970.

—————— Technics and Civilization. Harcourt, Brace and Company, 1934.

Murray, Thomas E., "Morality and Security—The Forgotten Equation," America, Vol. XCVI, No. 9 (Dec. 1, 1956), pp. 258–262.

—————— Nuclear Policy for War and Peace. The World Publishing Company, 1960.

Nagle, William J. (ed.), Morality and Modern Warfare: The State of the Question. Helicon Press, 1960.

O'Brien, William V., Nuclear War, Deterrence, and Morality. The Newman Press, 1967.

Orwell, George, "Politics and the English Language," in Orwell, George, Collected Essays. London: Mercury Books, 1961.

Poppy, John, "Violence: We Can End It," Look, Vol. XXXIII, No. 12 (June 10, 1969), pp. 21–23.

Potter, Ralph, War and Moral Discourse. John Knox Press, 1969.

Ramsey, Paul, The Just War: Force and Political Responsibility. Charles Scribner's Sons, 1968.

—————— War and the Christian Conscience: How Shall Modern War Be Conducted Justly? Duke University Press, 1961.

Rapoport, Anatol, Strategy and Conscience. Harper & Row, Publishers, 1964.

Raser, John R., "The Failure of Failsafe," Trans-action, Vol. VI, No. 3 (Jan. 1969), pp. 11–19.

Roszak, Theodore, The Making of a Counter Culture: Reflections on the Technocratic Society and Its Youthful Opposition. Doubleday & Company, Inc., 1968.

Schell, Orville, "The B-52—One of History's Most Indiscriminate and Destructive Weapons," *The Boston Globe*, May 31, 1971.

———— "The B-52 Stratofortress: U.S. War-Horse in Action," *American Report*, April 21, 1972.

———— "Electronic Death," *Christianity and Crisis*, Vol. XXXII, No. 8 (May 15, 1972), pp. 121–122.

Shaw, George Bernard, "Man and Superman," *Bernard Shaw, Selected Plays with Prefaces*, Vol. III. Dodd, Mead & Company, Inc., 1898.

Sibley, Mulford, *Unilateral Initiatives and Disarmament.* A Study and Commentary in the Beyond Deterrence Series. American Friends Service Committee, n.d.

Slater, Philip, *The Pursuit of Loneliness: American Culture at the Breaking Point.* Beacon Press, Inc., 1970.

Stackhouse, Max L., *The Ethics of Necropolis: An Essay on the Military-Industrial Complex and the Quest for a Just Peace.* Beacon Press, Inc., 1971.

Stein, Walter (ed.), *Nuclear Weapons: A Catholic Response.* Sheed & Ward, Inc., 1961.

Storr, Anthony, *Human Aggression.* Atheneum Publishers, 1968.

Waskow, Arthur I., *The Limits of Defense.* Doubleday & Company, Inc., 1962.

———— *Unintended War.* A Study and Commentary in the Beyond Deterrence Series. American Friends Service Committee, 1962.

———— (ed.), *The Debate Over Thermonuclear Strategy.* Problems in American Civilization. D. C. Heath & Company, 1965.

Weisberg, Barry (ed.), *Ecocide in Indochina: The Ecology of War.* Harper & Row, Publishers, Inc. 1970.

Weiss, George L., "The Air Force's Secret Electronic War," *Military Aircraft*, 1971.

Wells, Donald A., *The War Myth.* Pegasus, 1967.

Westmoreland, William C., Address to the Association of the United States Army, Oct. 14, 1969.

Wieman, Henry Nelson, *Religious Inquiry: Some Explorations.* Beacon Press, Inc., 1968.